STUDENT UNIT GUIDE

UNIT

AQA AS

Law

Law Making and the Legal System

Ian Yule and Peter Darwent

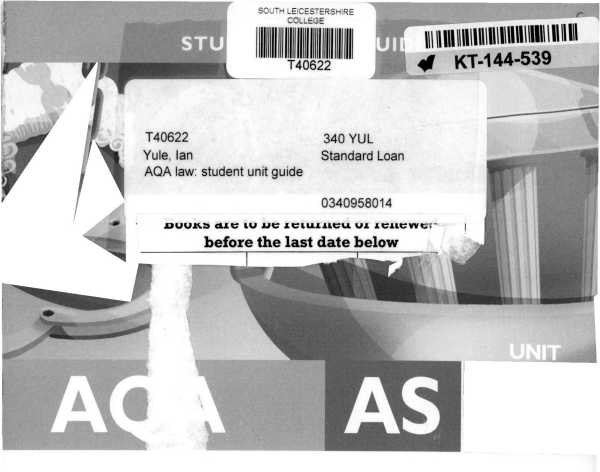

Philip Allan Updates, an imprint of Hodder Education, an Hachette UK company, Market Place, Deddington, Oxfordshire OX15 0SE

Orders
Bookpoint Ltd, 130 Milton Park, Abingdon, Oxfordshire OX14 4SB
tel: 01235 827720
fax: 01235 400454
e-mail: uk.orders@bookpoint.co.uk
Lines are open 9.00 a.m.–5.00 p.m., Monday to Saturday, with a 24-hour message answering service. You can also order through the Philip Allan Updates website: www.philipallan.co.uk

© Philip Allan Updates 2008

ISBN 978-0-340-95801-8

First printed 2008
Impression number   5 4 3
Year   2013 2012 2011 2010

This guide has been written specifically to support students preparing for the AQA AS Law Unit 1 examination. The content has been neither approved nor endorsed by AQA and remains the sole responsibility of the authors.

Typeset by Phoenix Photosetting, Chatham, Kent
Printed by MPG Books, Bodmin

Hachette UK's policy is to use papers that are natural, renewable and recyclable products and made from wood grown in sustainable forests. The logging and manufacturing processes are expected to conform to the environmental regulations of the country of origin.

Barcode	Date
140622	22/09/10

Class No.
340
Yuc

Contents

Introduction

About this guide

The AQA specification for the AS and A2 Law examinations is divided into four units. AS Unit 1 deals with **law making** and **the legal system**. The topics within this part of the specification are designed to provide a sound introduction to the way the English legal system works; they cover the different types of courts and the alternatives to courts, lawyers, judges, the particular importance of lay people, and the ways in which access to justice is ensured.

There are three sections to this guide:
- **Introduction** — this contains advice on how the guide should be used, an explanation of the skills required to complete the unit successfully and guidance on revision techniques.
- **Content Guidance** — this sets out the specification content for Unit 1, breaking it down into manageable sections for study and learning. It also contains references to cases that you need to study for a sound understanding of each topic.
- **Questions and Answers** — this provides 12 sample AS questions. All questions are followed by an A-grade answer; some of them are also followed by a C-grade answer. An examiner's comments show how marks are awarded or why they are withheld.

How to use this guide

While the Content Guidance covers all the elements of the Unit 1 specification, it is not intended to be a comprehensive and detailed set of notes for the unit — the material needs to be supplemented by further reading from textbooks and case studies.

At the end of each section, make a summary of the factual material under the appropriate headings, incorporating additional material from your wider reading and research, and then test yourself by using the sample question(s) on that particular topic. By practising questions and assessing your answers against the examiner's comments, you will learn how to use your knowledge and understanding effectively to improve your exam grade.

Learning strategies

It is essential to build up a good set of notes for successful AS study. Your notes need to be laid out clearly under headings, as in the Content Guidance section. They should contain accurate definitions, using the correct legal terminology, detailed explanation and relevant case and statutory references. It is recommended that you compile summaries of the most important cases.

Revision planning

At this level of study, it is essential that you understand the need to learn the basic factual information thoroughly as the module is being taught. Do not leave it to the revision stage, otherwise you will find that there is simply too much detailed knowledge to absorb — there is a real danger that facts from different sections will become confused (frequently a cause of problems in candidates' examination answers).

The word 'revise' is defined in the *Concise Oxford Dictionary* as to 'read again (work learned or done) to improve one's knowledge'. Simply skimming over some notes or reading this guide is *not* revision if you have not already learned the material.

The first stage of successful revision requires organisation of all your work. You should ensure that:
- your class notes are up to date
- you have used the material in this guide effectively
- you have made accurate notes on any wider reading, especially of case studies

The final key stage is to prepare a summary of all the material, organised under the headings and subheadings within the unit specification. The revision period is the time for going over all your notes and reducing them to manageable proportions, which is, in itself, an effective learning exercise. The act of summarising makes it easier to recall the material and should reduce the chance of forgetting parts of it in the examination. The greatest number of marks are lost not through factual mistakes but by simply omitting material or explanation.

Assessment objectives

Assessment objectives (AOs) are common to AS and A2 units and are intended to assess candidates' ability to:
- recall, select, deploy and develop knowledge and understanding of legal principles accurately and by means of examples
- analyse legal material, issues and situations, and evaluate and apply the appropriate legal rules and principles
- present a logical and coherent argument and communicate relevant material in a clear and effective manner, using correct legal terminology

Content Guidance

The specification for Unit 1 outlined in this section covers the following topics.

Section A: law making

Parliamentary law making

- Influences on Parliament: the role of the Law Commission; political, media and pressure group influences; Green and White Papers.
- The formal UK legislative process: the roles of the House of Commons, the House of Lords and the Crown; types of bill.
- The doctrine of parliamentary supremacy and its limitations.
- The effect of membership of the European Union and the Human Rights Act 1998.
- The advantages and disadvantages of influences on Parliament and of parliamentary law making.

Delegated legislation

- Types of delegated legislation and reasons for delegating powers.
- Parliamentary and judicial controls over delegated legislation.
- Advantages and disadvantages of delegated legislation.

Statutory interpretation

- Approaches to interpretation: literal, golden and mischief rules; purposive approach.
- Aids to interpretation and rules of language.
- Advantages and disadvantages of the different approaches and aids to statutory interpretation.

Judicial precedent

- The doctrine of precedent: court hierarchy; *stare decisis*, *ratio decidendi* and *obiter dicta*; law reports.
- Operation of the doctrine: following, overruling, distinguishing and disapproving.
- Advantages and disadvantages of the doctrine and operation of precedent.

Section B: the legal system

The courts system

- Civil courts and appeal system.
- Advantages and disadvantages of the civil courts.
- Criminal courts and appeal system.
- Classification of offences.

Alternatives to courts

- Functions of tribunals and arbitration; mediation, conciliation and negotiation.
- Comparison of these alternatives with each other and with civil courts in terms of cost, time, formality, representation, accessibility and appropriateness for particular kinds of dispute resolution.

Lay people
- Juries: qualifications, selection and role of jurors.
- Magistrates: selection and appointment; training; role and powers.
- Advantages and disadvantages of using lay people in the criminal courts.

Legal professions
- Barristers, solicitors and legal executives: qualifications, training and role.

Finance of advice and representation
- Private financing, insurance, 'law for free', conditional fee agreements.
- The statutory provision of legal help and representation in both civil and criminal cases; the Community Legal Service and Criminal Defence Service.
- Alternative sources of advice, e.g. Citizens Advice Bureaux.

The judiciary
- Qualifications; selection and appointment; training; functions in different types of court; dismissal procedures.
- Judicial independence.

Parliamentary law making

UK legislation consists of Acts of Parliament, which are also known as statutes. It is the result of a process involving the House of Commons, the House of Lords and the monarch (the queen). Statutes are referred to as **primary legislation**. Most legislation is drawn up (drafted) by the government.

The House of Commons is made up of Members of Parliament (MPs), elected to represent the people in their individual local constituencies. The political party that has the majority of seats forms the government of the day. The House of Lords, which is unelected, consists (at the time of writing) of 91 hereditary peers, with the rest of the House being life peers appointed by the government, Law Lords and senior bishops.

How statutes are created

All Acts of Parliament begin life as bills, of which there are two types: public bills and private bills.

Public bills

Public bills are by far the most common and they can be subdivided into government bills and private members' bills.

Government bills are introduced and piloted through the parliamentary process by a government minister. Some are controversial and reflect the views of the political party in power, such as the bills to privatise public utilities under the Conservative governments of Margaret Thatcher and John Major; others are concerned simply with the smooth running of the country, such as the **Access to Justice Act 1999**. There are some 40 to 50 government bills each year, most of which become law.

Before a bill is drawn up, the government department involved in the proposed changes to the law may issue a consultative document known as a **Green Paper**, setting out the proposals and allowing interested parties to comment on them. Any necessary changes can then be made and the final proposals set out in a **White Paper**. For example, the **Court and Legal Services Act 1990** was preceded by three Green Papers published in January 1989 and a White Paper ('Legal services: a framework for the future') published in July 1989, which set out the then government's proposals in relation to legal services generally. The bill is drawn up by parliamentary counsel, specialist lawyers in drafting bills, on the instructions of the relevant government department. They aim to make sure that the proposed law is worded exactly to give the intended result, but they are not always successful. Any ambiguous or misleading wording may lead to problems in the future and to judges having to rule on the interpretation of the relevant section.

Private members' bills are introduced by backbench MPs, whose names have been selected by ballot (20 each year). The choice of subject is their own but, as time for debate on these bills is limited, few become law. Success rates vary considerably from year to year. For example, in the 1996–97 session 26% of private members' bills were successful, whereas in 2002–03 just 13% were. In 2000–01, none reached the Statute Book.

To be successful, a private member's bill needs to have the tacit support of the government of the day. A good example is the **Abortion Act 1967**, which resulted from David Steel's private members' bill and with which the Labour government sympathised. Other examples of private members' bills that have become law include the **Murder (Abolition of Death Penalty) Act 1965**, the **Marriage Act 1994**, which allowed buildings other than register offices or places of worship to be used to conduct marriages, and the **Computer Misuse Act 1990**.

Private bills

Private bills are usually put forward by a local authority, public corporation or large public company and only affect the bodies concerned. A recent example is the **Medway Council Act 2004**, which gave Medway Council more power to control street trading in the borough.

There are also hybrid bills, which, when they become statutes, alter the general law but particularly affect the legal rights of a small number of people. The **Channel Tunnel Act 1987** is a good example.

Process of a bill through Parliament

A bill cannot become an Act of Parliament until it has been passed by both Houses of Parliament. The procedure consists of a number of stages and may commence in either the House of Commons or the House of Lords, although finance bills must begin in the House of Commons.

First reading
This takes place when the title of the bill is read out to the House.

Second reading
This crucial stage allows the House to hold a full debate on the main principles of the bill. At the end of the debate, a vote is taken as to whether the bill should proceed further.

Committee stage
If the vote is in favour, the bill passes to the committee stage. This involves a detailed examination of each clause of the bill by a standing committee of between 16 and 50 MPs. They will probably propose amendments to various clauses of the bill. Some amendments are put forward by opponents of the bill and are often politically motivated, but many are of a technical nature, designed to improve the bill.

Report stage
The committee reports back to the House on any amendments that have been made. These are debated and voted on.

Third reading
The bill is presented again to the House and the final vote is taken.

Passage through the other House
If the bill was introduced in the House of Commons, it then passes to the House of Lords (or vice versa), where the same procedure is repeated. If the House of Lords makes amendments to a bill that has already passed through the House of Commons, the bill is referred back to the Commons to consider the amendments.

Royal assent
Once a bill has passed successfully through all the stages in both Houses, it has to receive formal consent of the monarch in order to become law. This is known as royal assent.

Some Acts of Parliament come into force when royal assent is given, but most start on a specific date, which may be stated in the Act. Sometimes, different parts of the Act may come into effect at different times, which can cause uncertainty, as it can be difficult to find out which sections are in force.

Usually the legislative process takes several months to complete, especially if the proposals are controversial. On some occasions, however, if all the parties agree that a new law is needed urgently, an Act may be passed in 24 hours, such as the **Northern Ireland Bill 1972**.

Role of the House of Commons

Because the House of Commons is the elected body, it has the most important role in the law-making process. All important legislation begins in the House of Commons and all finance bills must start there.

By using the Parliament Acts, the Commons can defeat any attempt by the Lords to oppose a measure that the Commons has passed. In practice, this power is rarely used and the Commons often has to compromise in order to get legislation through. Because the Lords can delay a bill for a year, it has considerably more influence over the Commons during the last year of a Parliament's life.

In practice, any bill that the Commons passes will be either a government bill or a private members' bill that the government supports. The House of Commons is therefore not a truly independent body. In most cases, it does what the government tells it to do, because a majority of MPs are members of the governing party and pressured by the whips into supporting government bills.

Role of the House of Lords

Bills can start life in the House of Lords, though most begin in the Commons. Usually the legislation that starts in the Lords is not politically controversial or has a legal subject matter, for example the **Access to Justice Act 1999**. Occasionally, more controversial legislation can start in the House of Lords. This happened with the **Human**

Rights Act 1998, which was introduced for the government by the Lord Chancellor, who was a peer rather than an MP.

However, the House of Lords is primarily a revising and debating chamber, and it allows further detailed scrutiny of bills that have already passed through the House of Commons.

At times, the House of Lords has made the government rethink its proposals. For example, in March 2005 it forced the government to amend its plans in the **Terrorism Bill** for control orders to deal with terrorist suspects.

The unelected House of Lords used to be able to prevent legislation put forward by the elected House of Commons, as the agreement of both Houses was necessary. This power is restricted by the **Parliament Acts 1911 and 1949**. If the House of Lords rejects a bill, it can still become law, provided it is reintroduced to the House of Commons in the next parliamentary session and passes all the stages again. The Lords are not allowed to delay finance bills.

This power to force the Lords to pass a bill has only been used five times — for example to push through the **War Crimes Act 1991** and the **Hunting Act 2004**.

Usually, a government threat to use the Parliament Acts is enough. Initially, the Lords rejected the lowering of the homosexual age of consent from 18 to 16 when this was introduced as part of the **Crime and Disorder Bill 1998**, but in 2000 a new bill was introduced, and after the government made it clear that it would invoke the Parliament Acts, the House of Lords gave in.

Role of the Crown

The Crown plays a purely formal role, and any attempt by a monarch to thwart the will of the Commons and Lords would not be tolerated. Since Queen Anne refused to pass the **Scotch Militia Bill 1707**, no monarch has refused to assent to a bill.

Advantages of the UK law-making system

- The House of Commons is an elected body. MPs are answerable to the voters and there must be an election at least every 5 years. The Commons can, if necessary, force its will on the Lords by using the Parliament Acts.
- Parliament takes note of public opinion. While a bill is going through Parliament, there are opportunities for people to lobby and express their views. The decision of the House of Commons in February 2006 to vote for a complete ban on smoking in public places could be seen as Parliament responding to public opinion.
- The House of Lords is not elected, so it is less concerned with staying popular with voters. It can therefore be a useful check on a government that has a large majority in the Commons.
- There are many people in the Lords who have specialist expertise, for example lawyers, doctors and scientists, or who have been successful in running companies or charities. These people bring practical knowledge and experience to their examination of bills.

- The legislative process is thorough, with detailed committee examination of bills in both Houses as well as general debates.
- Delegated legislation means that much of the detail can be left to government departments to draw up through statutory instruments.
- When it is necessary, an Act can be passed quickly. For example, the **Criminal Justice (Terrorism and Conspiracy) Act 1998** went through all its stages in 2 days, and the **Northern Ireland Bill 1972** was passed in just 24 hours.

Disadvantages of the UK law-making system

- There is not enough time to pass all the legislation that is necessary, and reform bills (e.g. to modernise the law on non-fatal offences) are often left out of the government's legislative programme.
- Because the government usually has a comfortable majority in the Commons, it is difficult for Parliament to influence or change what the government wants. For example, several aspects of the **Criminal Justice and Public Order Act 1994** were criticised, yet no changes were made during its passage through Parliament.
- There is inadequate scrutiny of legislation. The government controls the parliamentary timetable, and through processes such as the guillotine it can restrict discussion of a bill. Also, because the government has a majority on all the standing committees, it is able to defeat any amendments put forward in committee. H. W. R. Wade argues that 'the most shocking feature of our legislative process is the way in which parliamentary scrutiny is eliminated on the pretext of shortage of time'.
- Some bills are passed too quickly, usually in response to a real or imagined emergency. The **Dangerous Dogs Act 1991** was described by a judge in one case as bearing 'all the hallmarks of an ill-thought-out piece of legislation, no doubt in hasty response to yet another strident pressure group'.
- The House of Lords, which is not elected, is able to delay legislation that the House of Commons has passed. No other democratic country has an unelected second chamber able to frustrate the decisions of an elected body in this way.
- The original proposals in a bill can be amended, often more than once. This can result in the final legislation being unclear in some areas and having to be interpreted later by the courts.

Doctrine of parliamentary supremacy

Parliamentary supremacy (sovereignty) is a fundamental part of the UK constitution. It means that as a democratically elected body, Parliament is the supreme law-making body in the country. A. V. Dicey, the nineteenth-century jurist, stated: 'Parliament has the right to make or unmake any law whatever; and, further...no person or body is recognised by the law of England as having a right to override or set aside the legislation of Parliament.' In practice, it means that Acts of Parliament passed using the proper procedures cannot be challenged. They must be applied by the courts and override any judicial precedent, delegated legislation or previous Act of Parliament that covers that area of law. Parliament also has the power to rescind (unmake) any law it has passed.

Another aspect is the idea that no Parliament can bind its successors (i.e. no Parliament can make laws that will restrict law making in future Parliaments). Acts of Parliament can also apply retrospectively (i.e. to past events) and extra-territorially (i.e. to events outside the UK). An Act combining both these elements was the **War Crimes Act 1991**, which allowed the prosecution of people for crimes committed in Europe during the Second World War.

Limitations on sovereignty

Public opinion

There have always been practical limits to what Parliament can do. All politicians are sensitive to public opinion and plans for law making are likely to reflect this.

Entrenched laws

There are entrenched laws, which deal with fundamental constitutional issues and which would be difficult for any future Parliament to change, for example legislation extending voting rights to women and lowering the voting age to 18. Another example is the more recent granting of legislative powers to a Scottish Parliament.

Membership of the European Union (EU)

Under the Treaty of Rome 1957, European Community law, enacted by the powers set out in treaties, takes priority over conflicting laws in member states. (To become binding, treaties have to be ratified by all member states, and at the time of writing it is uncertain whether the Treaty of Lisbon will come into effect after its rejection by Ireland in a referendum in June 2008.) The **European Communities Act 1972** incorporates this principle into UK law. Even if Parliament passes an Act that conflicts with EU law, EU law must prevail, as shown in the *Factortame* case in 1990. For areas of law not covered by the EU, Parliament is supreme.

Human Rights Act 1998

This came into force in October 2000 and incorporates the European Convention on Human Rights into English law. Under the Act, the Convention does not have superiority over English law and Parliament can still make laws that conflict with it. However, under s.19 of the Act, all bills require a statement from a government minister before the second reading in each House, saying that the provisions of the bill are compatible with the Convention or, if not, that the government nevertheless intends the bill to proceed.

Under s.3 of the Act, the courts are required as far as possible to interpret Acts so that they comply with the Convention. If an Act cannot be reconciled with the Convention, a judge can make a declaration of incompatibility, although ministers are not obliged to change the law. It could be argued that because Parliament can refuse to respond to a declaration by a judge that an Act is incompatible with the Convention, the doctrine of parliamentary supremacy is unaffected. However, it is clearly significant that judges can challenge the validity of Acts of Parliament, and in practice it is likely that a government will accept that the legislation has to change.

Influences on Parliament

In order to be effective, the law must be able to adapt to changes in society, so the law-making process has to be ongoing. There are many pressures on Parliament that try to influence the direction of this process, ranging from political considerations such as the party manifesto to law reform agencies or other pressure/interest groups.

Exam questions may ask you to describe a number of the influences on Parliament. Sometimes they specify the number (e.g. three). You will always have to give examples of their influence. You may also be asked to comment on advantages and disadvantages.

Political pressures

When a general election is to be held, each political party presents a **party manifesto**, setting out its proposals for new legislation if elected into government. These have covered such things as the right to buy council houses, included in the Conservative Party's 1979 manifesto and implemented through the **Housing Act 1980**. The **Human Rights Act 1998**, which implemented the Labour Party's manifesto commitment to incorporate the European Convention on Human Rights into English law, and the **House of Lords Act 1999**, which greatly reduced the number of hereditary peers, were also the result of manifesto commitments.

Some bills are responses to particular and unexpected events, such as the **Prevention of Terrorism (Temporary Provisions) Act 1974** in response to the Birmingham IRA bombings, or the **Drought Act 1976**, which was introduced to deal with a serious drought in the summer of 1976.

Membership of the EU is another influence, as it creates obligations under the treaties whereby decisions made by the EU Commission or Council of Ministers must be enacted as new laws. For example, the **Consumer Protection Act 1987** was passed to give effect to the Product Liability Directive, which imposes strict liability on producers for damage caused by their products.

The civil service in each ministerial department also has its own views as to the legislation necessary to achieve its goals.

Advantages of political influences
- Governments are elected and they usually respond to what the public wants. They wish to be re-elected, so it is unlikely they will pass unpopular Acts.
- It is helpful that when there is an emergency, the government can respond quickly and use its influence over Parliament to pass appropriate emergency measures. The **Anti-terrorism, Crime and Security Act 2001** is an example.
- Parliament is also flexible enough to respond to other political influences. Individual MPs have been responsible for valuable reforms, such as the abolition of the death penalty and the regulation of minicabs in London.
- Governmental ideas for legislation are thought out and planned with the help of expert civil servants. The civil servants have to implement the new laws, so it is likely that they will have thought about any problems.

Disadvantages of political influences

- Governments want to be popular, so they are reluctant to introduce laws that are necessary but unpopular, such as tougher rules on speeding or on drinking and driving.
- Because they are concerned with being re-elected, governments concentrate on passing laws that will make them popular. As a result, necessary but non-urgent law reforms, such as improving the law on non-fatal offences, are neglected.
- The government usually gets its way if it has a large majority in the House of Commons. This can give the impression that Parliament is weak and largely ineffective in modifying government proposals.

Pressure groups

Pressure groups are bodies of people with a shared interest in getting the government to change the law in certain areas. They include groups such as Shelter, Help the Aged, Greenpeace, Friends of the Earth, trade unions, business groups such as the Confederation of British Industry and professional organisations such as the Law Society.

They target politicians, civil servants and local government offices by lobbying MPs, organising petitions and gaining as much publicity as possible for their cause. Well-organised groups, such as Greenpeace and Friends of the Earth, have been successful. Governments now have to consider the environmental impact of their policies because of heightened public awareness of environmental issues. Shelter was successful in persuading the government to introduce change for homeless people in the **Housing Homeless Persons Act 1977**. At times, groups may join forces to get their point across to the government. This happened when people opposed to the banning of fox hunting held a joint march in London with the Countryside Alliance.

Large groups are often more successful than smaller ones, but sometimes one person can bring about change almost single-handedly. The late Mary Whitehouse headed a campaign against child pornography, which led the government to introduce the **Protection of Children Act 1984**.

Some pressure groups exist only for a short time, as they are set up to deal with a specific issue, for instance a campaign about a proposed bypass. The group disbands once the issue is resolved. An example is the National Campaign for the Abolition of Capital Punishment, which was set up in 1955 and disbanded in 1969 when the suspension of the death penalty was made permanent.

Sometimes a pressure group is set up as a result of a tragic event. The Snowdrop Campaign, organised after the Dunblane massacre in 1996, resulted in Parliament banning the private ownership of most types of handguns.

Sectional or interest groups exist to further the ends of their own particular section of society. Examples are trade unions, groups such as the National Farmers' Union (NFU) or the Confederation of British Industry (CBI), and professional associations such as the British Medical Association and the Law Society.

The degree of influence exercised by such groups varies. Trade unions traditionally have more power under Labour governments, while their importance declined sharply during the Conservative governments from 1979 to 1997. Groups such as the CBI and the NFU would expect to be consulted by governments of all political persuasions, though traditionally they have more influence under Conservative governments.

Professional associations representing groups such as lawyers and doctors, made up of well-educated, articulate and often wealthy individuals, are influential, and governments of all parties would tend to consult them before introducing a bill affecting their interests. For example, the Law Society, which represents solicitors, has a parliamentary unit that actively lobbies MPs and peers from all parties for changes in the law.

Advantages of pressure groups

- Pressure groups give the public and particularly minorities a voice. They act as a safety valve for frustrations, as in pro-hunting and anti-Iraq War protests.
- They help MPs keep in touch with what people think. For example, pressure from environmental groups may have persuaded the government to change car tax regulations to favour smaller, more fuel-efficient cars.
- They raise public awareness of issues that affect their interest or cause. For example, Fathers 4 Justice has been successful through a variety of stunts in raising awareness of the plight of many fathers denied access to their children after a divorce.
- Members of pressure groups often have considerable expertise and can therefore suggest detailed and well-thought-out law changes. Many groups have draft bills ready for backbench MPs to introduce.

Disadvantages of pressure groups

- Some large pressure groups that represent powerful organisations are extremely influential, and it is difficult for smaller pressure groups to match their influence. Environmental groups claim that the strength of the road lobby and the airline industry means that new roads or airport extensions are difficult to fight.
- The methods of some pressure groups can be a problem, for example strikes and protests can cause disruption, such as the blockading of oil depots. The direct-action tactics of Fathers 4 Justice have been criticised. Members of the Countryside Alliance broke into the House of Commons as part of its campaign in favour of fox hunting. Extremist groups, such as animal rights activists, may even break the law by attacking scientific laboratories and the homes and property of individual employees of drug companies.
- Even if an interest or pressure group does manage to present its arguments, this does not mean that its views will be taken into consideration.

The media

The media include television, radio, newspapers and journals, and they play a powerful role in bringing issues to the attention of the government. Newspapers in particular promote specific issues or causes. For example, the *Daily Mail* has often run headlines on immigration or asylum issues in order to try to achieve tighter controls, and the *Sun* has consistently campaigned against what it sees as the growing influence of the EU on

British life. Another example of media influence was the campaign run by the *News of the World* in 2000 following the murder of Sarah Payne by a paedophile. It published details of known paedophiles in order to force the government to take action. The result was a register of sex offenders and the promise of much closer supervision of those released into the community.

Advantages of the media
- The media play a powerful role in bringing issues to the attention of the government and can force it to act.
- Coverage in newspapers and on television and radio can raise the public profile of an issue and add weight to public opinion.

Disadvantages of the media
- It is a concern that ownership of British newspapers and other branches of the media is in the hands of a relatively small number of individuals. Newspapers often adopt views that reflect those of their owners. Rupert Murdoch, who owns the *Sun,* the *News of the World*, *The Times*, the *Sunday Times* and Sky television, has used his newspapers to project his own views, particularly his strong opposition to the EU.
- The media have a tendency to create panics by drawing attention to and often exaggerating issues, such as the activities of paedophiles. In some cases, the media whip up public opinion instead of reflecting it.

Law reform agencies

The most important of these today is the Law Commission, but in the past specialist bodies such as the Criminal Law Revision Committee were important (the **Theft Acts** of **1968 and 1978** resulted from its work).

There are also temporary committees that are set up to review a specific area of law. They are usually referred to by the name of their chairperson, for example the Royal Commission on Criminal Justice 1993 was known as the 'Runciman Commission'. Their job is complete when they have made their report.

The Law Commission
This was established by the **Law Commission Act 1965**. It is a full-time body with five Commissioners. The chairperson is a High Court judge and the other four are from the legal professions and academic lawyers. Their members of staff are all legally trained. The Commission's work involves looking at reform of the law, codification and consolidation.

The Commission may have topics referred to it by the Lord Chancellor and government departments, or may select a topic of its own, which will be considered after government approval has been gained.

After researching a selected area of law, the Commission produces a consultative paper that details the present law, setting out the problems and options for change. The views of interested parties are sought, after which a final report is published, setting out recommendations and, if legislation is proposed, a draft bill. This will only become law if it goes through the full parliamentary process. Legislation that has resulted from this process includes the **Law Reform (Year and a Day Rule) Act 1996** and the **Contract (Rights of Third Parties) Act 1999**.

The success of the Law Commission in achieving law reform has varied. Initially, there was a high success rate in getting its proposals accepted and enacted, but this has not been maintained. During 1994–95, improvements were brought about by the introduction of new parliamentary procedures. However, in recent years the backlog of proposals has increased again. In 2003–04, the Law Commission reported that seven proposals had been made law, but a further 17 were awaiting parliamentary time and 13 were waiting for a government decision.

Another aim of the Law Commission is to codify the law in certain areas, but this has not been achieved. The Draft Criminal Code was published in 1985 but has never become law. The arguments in favour of codification are that it will make the law accessible and understandable, and provide consistency and certainty. People would be able to know what the law is as it is contained in one place. The arguments against codification are that a detailed code would make the law too rigid, but if it is insufficiently detailed it will need to be interpreted by the courts, creating uncertainty. Therefore, the Commission has selected areas of law and clarified them, hoping to codify them at a later date if possible.

Consolidation involves drawing together all the provisions set out in a number of statutes, so that they are all in one Act. About five consolidation bills are produced each year. A problem with this is that even when the area of law is consolidated, further Acts of Parliament can change it again. The **Powers of the Criminal Courts (Sentencing) Act 2000** was changed by the **Criminal Justice and Courts Act 2000**, where community sentences were renamed and new powers of sentencing created.

Advantages of the Law Commission
- It is made up of lawyers with much expertise, headed by a High Court judge. The Commissioners change every 5 years, so a different range of views is brought into the law-reform process.
- It is a permanent, full-time body and can investigate any areas of law it thinks needs to be reformed.
- It produces draft bills ready for Parliament to introduce, which reduces the workload for ministers.
- It has been responsible for many sensible changes to the law, for example the **Unfair Contract Terms Act 1977** and the abolition of the 'Year and a Day' rule.
- It can undertake extensive research and engage in wide consultation, so its recommendations for law reform are well informed and this helps to avoid problems in the application of the law.

Disadvantages of the Law Commission
- Parliament has often ignored the Commission's proposals. Up until 1999, only two-thirds of its proposals had been implemented.
- Sometimes, because its recommendations are usually balanced and measured, they may not suit the political agenda of the government of the day.

- Often governments cannot find time in the legislative programme for non-urgent law reform. The present Labour government accepted the proposals for reform to the law on non-fatal offences, and the Home Office even produced a draft bill in 1998, but this has proceeded no further.
- The Law Commission investigates as many as 20–30 areas at the same time. This may mean that each investigation is not as thorough as one carried out by a Royal Commission or a Commission of Inquiry.

Delegated legislation

Delegated legislation (secondary legislation) is law that is not made by Parliament but that has its authority. Parliament, in many cases in a statute, may create a framework of law. Authority (permission) is usually given in a 'parent' Act of Parliament known as an **enabling Act**. This Act creates the framework of the law and then delegates power to others to make more detailed law in that area. Examples of enabling Acts are the **Local Government Act 1972**, which allows local authorities such as district and county councils to make bylaws, and the **Access to Justice Act 1999**, which gives the Lord Chancellor wide powers to alter aspects of the system of state funding for legal cases.

Types of delegated legislation

Orders in Council

Orders in Council are made by the Privy Council and can be used for a wide variety of purposes, for example the regulation of certain professional bodies. They are used when an ordinary statutory instrument would be inappropriate, for instance when transferring responsibilities between government departments. Orders in Council were used to transfer powers from ministers of the UK government to ministers of the devolved assemblies.

In times of emergency, when Parliament is not sitting, the queen and Privy Council may make an Order in Council under the **Emergency Powers Act 1920**. These powers were used during the foot-and-mouth crisis in 2001, when decisions needed to be made quickly to try to prevent the spread of the disease. They were also used during the fuel crisis of 2000.

Statutory instruments

This is the most common type of delegated legislation. There were 3,662 statutory instruments made in 2007. Authority is given to ministers and government departments to make these regulations for their area of responsibility, for example the Minister of Transport has the power under various Road Traffic Acts to make detailed road traffic regulations.

Regulations are a good way of updating primary legislation and adapting the law to changing circumstances. For example, the **Health and Safety at Work Act 1974** has been updated through the **Management of Health and Safety at Work Regulations 1992**.

Statutory instruments are used to implement European Union directives in English law. An example is the **Unfair Terms in Consumer Contracts Regulations 1994**, which implemented a directive aimed at giving greater protection to consumers.

They are also used to bring an Act of Parliament, or parts of it, into effect by means of a Commencement Order.

Bylaws

Parliament has given local authorities and other public bodies the right to make law in certain areas. Local authorities, such as county councils, district councils and parish councils, can make bylaws to cover such things as parking restrictions and banning the drinking of alcohol in certain public places. The introduction of the congestion charge zone in central London is an example.

Public corporations and certain companies can also make bylaws to help to enforce rules concerning public behaviour; the London Underground's ban on smoking is an example. All bylaws must be approved by the relevant government minister.

Professional regulations

Professional regulations also come under the heading of delegated legislation, such as those found in the **Solicitors Act 1974** empowering the Law Society to regulate the conduct of its members.

Control of delegated legislation

Why do we need controls over delegated legislation?

Statistically, there is far more delegated legislation made per year than primary legislation. A great deal of legislation is therefore being made by persons and bodies other than Parliament, without being subject to the full scrutiny of the parliamentary process.

Because most delegated legislation is not made by elected bodies and many people have the power to create it, it is important to make sure that the power is not abused and is controlled. This can be done by Parliament or the courts.

Control by Parliament

Parliament has some control at the time an enabling Act is made, as it sets the limits for making delegated legislation under that Act.

In addition, the Delegated Powers Scrutiny Committee in the House of Lords can decide whether the provisions in a bill to delegate legislative power are inappropriate. Its report is presented to the House of Lords before the committee stage but it has no power to amend the bill.

Some enabling Acts require an **affirmative resolution** from Parliament before the delegated legislation can become law. The delegated legislation has to be laid before both Houses, and if a vote to approve it is taken within a specified time, it becomes law.

Much more delegated legislation is subject to a **negative resolution**. The delegated legislation is put before Parliament, and if no member has put down a motion to annul it within a specified period (usually 40 days) it becomes law.

The **Joint Committee on Statutory Instruments**, with members from both Houses of Parliament (the Scrutiny Committee), reviews all statutory instruments and can draw the attention of Parliament to any that need special consideration. A statutory instrument will be referred back to Parliament if:

- it imposes a tax
- under the Act the statutory instrument cannot be challenged in the courts
- the delegated legislation appears to be retrospectively effective and this was not provided for in the enabling Act
- the powers granted in the Act have been exceeded or used in an unusual way
- the legislation is defective or needs clarification

The Committee has no power to alter the legislation, as it merely reports back on its findings, but it does provide a check on delegated legislation. Parliament itself holds the ultimate safeguard, in that it can withdraw the delegated power and revoke any piece of delegated legislation at any time.

Control by the courts

Unlike a statute, the validity of delegated legislation can be challenged in the courts. Any individual who has a personal interest in the delegated legislation (i.e. who is affected by it) may apply to the courts under the **judicial review** procedure. The grounds for this is that they believe the piece of delegated legislation is *ultra vires*, which means that it goes beyond the powers granted by Parliament. If it is found to be *ultra vires,* the delegated legislation is declared void and ineffective.

This can be in the form of **procedural *ultra vires***, where a public authority has not followed the procedures set out in the enabling Act for creating delegated legislation. In *Agricultural, Horticultural and Forestry Training Board* v *Aylesbury Mushrooms Ltd* (1972), failure by the Minister of Labour to consult interested parties as required by the Act led to the order being declared invalid.

A claim of **substantive *ultra vires*** occurs where the delegated legislation goes beyond the powers granted by the enabling Act. In *R* v *Home Secretary ex parte Fire Brigades Union* (1995), where the home secretary made changes to the Criminal Injuries Compensation Scheme, he was held to have exceeded the power given in the **Criminal Justice Act 1988**. Another example is *R* v *Secretary of State for Health ex parte Pfizer* (1999), in which it was held that a circular from the secretary of state for health advising doctors not to prescribe Viagra went beyond the powers given in the parent Acts.

The courts will also declare invalid any delegated legislation that is unreasonable, under the principle established in *Associated Provincial Picture Houses* v *Wednesbury Corporation* (1948). This may be because the rules are unjust, are made in bad faith or are so perverse that no reasonable person would have made them.

Effectiveness of the controls on delegated legislation

There are drawbacks to control by Parliament. The use of the affirmative procedure usually draws Parliament's attention to the delegated legislation, but only on rare occasions is it possible to stop the legislation from being passed. The Scrutiny Committee is more important and has managed to have changes made to some pieces of delegated legislation. Its powers are limited, however, as it can only consider whether the delegated powers have been used correctly, and not the merits of the legislation. Its reports are not binding either.

Control by the courts has been successful in many cases, but there are limitations on judicial control. The delegated legislation may have been in force for years before someone affected by it is prepared to challenge it. Another problem is that the discretionary powers conferred on the minister by the enabling Act may be extremely wide, resulting in difficulties in establishing that he or she has acted *ultra vires*.

Advantages of delegated legislation

There are a number of reasons why delegated legislation is needed:

- There is not enough time for Parliament to consider every detail of every regulation/rule. More than 3,000 statutory instruments are passed every year, so delegated legislation allows Parliament to concentrate on broad issues of policy rather than masses of detail.
- Parliament does not have the knowledge or technical expertise necessary in certain areas, such as building regulations or health and safety regulations at work. Delegating legislation allows the use of experts in the relevant areas to make the rules.
- Local people know local needs. Local authority bylaws, as a result, are more appropriate than broad and general national legislation.
- Delegated legislation can be achieved more quickly than an Act of Parliament. It can also be amended more quickly if circumstances change, allowing flexibility.
- Delegated legislation is easily revoked if it causes problems. An Act of Parliament would require another statute to amend or revoke it, which would take much longer.
- It is impossible for Parliament to foresee all the problems that might arise when it passes a statute. When problems do arise, delegated legislation to rectify them can be put into place quickly.

Disadvantages of delegated legislation

- The main argument against delegated legislation is that it is undemocratic, because it is made by unelected people rather than by Parliament.
- Much is sub-delegated and made by civil servants in the relevant government departments rather than by the ministers who were originally given the delegated powers. Civil servants are unaccountable to the electorate. (This is not the case with bylaws, as local authorities are elected bodies and accountable to the voters in their area.)
- The large amount of delegated legislation makes it difficult to keep track of the current law. There is little publicity compared to that received by Acts of Parliament, so people may be unaware that a particular piece of legislation exists.
- Control by Parliament is not always effective. Few statutory instruments have affirmative resolution, and MPs are too busy to look at the others. Scrutiny Committee recommendations are often ignored.
- There can be a lack of scrutiny. It has been argued that delegated legislation can be used by governments to make quite significant changes to the law and avoid the inconvenience of submitting them to the scrutiny of the parliamentary process. This is particularly the case with 'Henry VIII clauses', which allow delegated legislation to be used to amend or repeal Acts of Parliament.

Statutory interpretation

The process of statutory interpretation is used by judges in the courts when there is a dispute or uncertainty over the meaning of a word or phrase in an Act of Parliament or piece of delegated legislation. The role of the courts is to find out how Parliament intended the law to apply and to carry out this interpretation. It may form a precedent for future cases. The necessity for this can arise for a number of reasons:

- Due to the complexity of the English language, a word may have several meanings, which can lead to ambiguity.
- The meaning of words can change over time.
- The legislation may have been drawn up quickly in response to public reaction and the wording may not be as precise as it should be. A good example is the **Dangerous Dogs Act 1991**, which, drawn up and enacted after a series of incidents during the late summer of 1989 caused great public concern, uses a broad term instead of a limited and specific word.
- The drafting of the original bill may have contained errors. Parliament may not notice errors, especially if there are many amendments during a bill's passage through all the parliamentary stages.
- Changes in technology and social issues can affect how an Act is applied, as in *Royal College of Nursing* v *DHSS* (1981).
- The amount of delegated legislation is increasing.

Aids to statutory interpretation

Judges can use various aids when interpreting a statute. These include internal or intrinsic aids, and external or extrinsic aids.

Internal or intrinsic aids

These are found in the Act itself and may help to make its meaning clear.

- **The long title and the short title of the Act**. In *Cornwall County Council* v *Baker* (2003), the divisional court referred to the long title to confirm the purpose of the **Protection of Animals (Amendment) Act 2000**.
- **The preamble**, if there is one. Older Acts have a detailed preamble outlining what the statute covered and its purpose.
- **Marginal notes and headings**. Some sections of the Act may have headings, and marginal notes are usually added by the person drafting the Act. Both may provide guidance. A marginal note was referred to in *R* v *Tivnan* (1999) in order to clarify whether it was Parliament's intention to deprive drug dealers of assets equivalent in value to the proceeds obtained from drug dealing, and not necessarily just those assets purchased directly from the proceeds of the drug dealing.
- **The interpretation section**. Most Acts now contain interpretation sections. An example is s.10 of the **Theft Act 1968**, which after referring to the use of 'a weapon of offence' in aggravated burglary, defines it as 'any article made or adapted for use for causing injury'.
- **Schedules**. Acts often contain schedules, which are found at the end of an Act and include more detailed clarification. An example is Schedule 2 of the **Unfair Contract Terms Act 1977**, which outlines the tests for determining the principle of reasonableness.

External or extrinsic aids

These are found outside the Act and include the following:

- **Dictionaries** of various kinds. For example, in *Vaughan* v *Vaughan* (1973), where a man had been pestering his ex-wife, the Court of Appeal used a dictionary in order to define 'molest' and concluded that the definition was wide enough to cover his behaviour.
- **Previous Acts of Parliament and earlier case law**. In *Royal Crown Derby Porcelain Co. Ltd* v *Raymond Russell* (1949), when considering the **Rent and Mortgage Act 1933**, the court interpreted words used in the Act by referring to similar words used in an earlier Act and to the interpretation applied to these words in a number of cases.
- **Reference to *Hansard***, the official report of the proceedings in Parliament. Until 1990, the courts were not allowed to refer to *Hansard* in order to find out Parliament's intention. This was overturned in *Pepper* v *Hart* (1993). However, this use is restricted to cases where the words of an Act are ambiguous or obscure or lead to an absurdity, and even then, only where there is a clear statement by the minister

introducing the legislation that would resolve the doubt. The wider use of *Hansard* is only permitted if the legislation in question has introduced an international convention or European directive into English law. In *Three Rivers DC* v *Bank of England* (1996), it was held that the *Pepper* v *Hart* principle did not have to be applied so narrowly because it was important to construe the statute purposively and consistently with any European materials such as directives.

- **Law reform reports** from bodies such as the Law Commission.
- **International treaties**. *Fothergill* v *Monarch Airlines Ltd* (1980) confirmed that *travaux préparatoires* (background working papers) could be used to ascertain the meaning of an ambiguous or doubtful section of an Act based on an international treaty.
- **Explanatory notes**. Since 1999, all government bills are accompanied by explanatory notes, which provide guidance on complex parts of the bill.

The rules of interpretation

Over the years, judges have developed different approaches to the problem of interpreting statutes. They are usually referred to as 'rules', but more accurately they are 'approaches' because judges are not compelled to follow them as they would be if they were rules. There are traditionally said to be three 'rules' used by judges in interpreting statutes: the literal rule, the golden rule and the mischief rule. There is also now the purposive approach, which is a development of the mischief rule.

The literal rule

This means giving words their plain, ordinary, dictionary meaning — no matter how unfortunate the consequences. Lord Reid in *Pinner* v *Everett* (1969) referred to 'the natural and ordinary meaning of that word or phrase in its context'.

The rule was used in *Whiteley* v *Chappell* (1868), where the defendant was charged with the offence of impersonating 'any person entitled to vote' at an election. The defendant was acquitted because he impersonated a dead person; applying the literal rule, a dead person is not entitled to vote. Another example is *Fisher* v *Bell* (1961), in which a shopkeeper put flick knives on display in his shop window. The **Restriction of Offensive Weapons Act 1959** made it an offence to sell flick knives or offer them for sale. However, the court decided that flick knives on display in a shop window were not an offer to sell but rather an invitation to treat. Therefore, despite the fact that Parliament had legislated to prevent just this sort of display, applying the literal rule meant that the defendant was not guilty, and Parliament had to amend the Act as a result of this case.

This rule has also led to unfair or unjust decisions. In *London and North Eastern Railway Co.* v *Berriman* (1946), Mrs Berriman was unable to obtain compensation when her husband was killed while carrying out maintenance work oiling points on the railway line. The relevant statute said that a lookout should be provided to warn rail workers of approaching trains when relaying or repairing the track; however, Berriman was 'maintaining' the tracks. The words 'relaying' and 'repairing' were given their literal meaning.

Despite Lord Denning's observation in *Nothman* v *London Borough of Barnet* (1978) that 'the literal method is now completely out of date', the literal rule is still used by judges. It was used in *Cutter* v *Eagle Star Insurance Co.* (1998), in which the House of Lords decided that the word 'road' in the **Road Traffic Act 1988** could not include a car park.

Advantages of the literal rule

- The main argument used to justify the rule is that it respects the sovereignty of Parliament and prevents unelected judges from making law. Viscount Simonds in *Magor and St Mellons RDC* v *Newport Corporation* (1952) argued that it was not open to judges to fill in gaps, as Lord Denning wanted, or otherwise alter statutes. If a gap was disclosed, 'the remedy lies in an amending Act'.
- People know where they stand with the literal rule because the wording will not change. It therefore encourages certainty, and, because there is less scope for interpretation, there is likely to be less litigation.
- It often leads to quick decisions because the answer can be found by referring to dictionaries, although this will only be the case when the words are clear and unambiguous.

Disadvantages of the literal rule

- Use of the literal rule can lead to unfair or unjust decisions, as for example in *London and North Eastern Railway Co.* v *Berriman* (1946). It can also lead to absurd decisions, which were clearly not what Parliament intended. Examples of this would be *Fisher* v *Bell* (1961) and *Whiteley* v *Chappell* (1868).
- Words may have more than one meaning, making it difficult to apply a dictionary definition.
- It is not always possible to word an Act so as to cover every situation. Circumstances may occur which were not anticipated by Parliament.
- Michael Zander says that the rule is mechanical and divorced from the realities of the use of language.
- As a 1969 report by the Law Commission, critical of the literal rule, stated, 'to place undue emphasis on the literal meaning of words is to assume an unattainable perfection in draftsmanship'.
- The literal rule gives judges little discretion to adapt the law to changing times.

The golden rule

This is a modification of the literal rule and says that judges should use the literal rule unless it would produce an absurd result. There are two views on how far the rule should be used: the narrow application and the wider application.

Under the **narrow application**, proposed by Lord Reid in *Jones* v *DPP* (1962), if a word is ambiguous the judge may choose between possible meanings of the word in order to avoid an absurd outcome. He argued that if a word had more than one meaning, 'then you can choose between those meanings, but beyond this you cannot go'.

This application was used in *R* v *Allen* (1872). Section 57 of the **Offences Against the Person Act 1861** made it an offence to marry if you were already married to someone else. The court decided that 'marry' was ambiguous and could have two meanings: to become legally married or to go through a ceremony of marriage. Allen sought to rely on the first definition and argued that since he was already married, his second marriage could not be valid, so he could not be guilty of bigamy. However, it was clearly absurd to apply the first meaning, as no one could then be convicted of the offence. Therefore, the judge chose the second meaning and Allen was found guilty.

The **wider application** is where there is only one meaning but this would lead to an absurd or repugnant situation. In *Adler* v *George* (1964), s.3 of **the Official Secrets Act 1920** made it an offence to be found 'in the vicinity of a prohibited place'. The accused was arrested *inside* the prohibited place; therefore, he argued that he could not be convicted. Lord Parker CJ used the golden rule and held that 'in the vicinity of' could mean 'being in or in the vicinity of' the prohibited place. Another example is *Re Sigsworth* (1935), in which the court prevented a son who had murdered his mother from inheriting his mother's estate under the intestacy rules set out in the **Administration of Estates Act 1925**. The wording of the Act was unambiguous, but the court did not want the murderer to benefit from his crime.

Advantages of the golden rule
- The courts can alter the wording and make sense of absurd or repugnant wording. *Re Sigsworth* concerned just such a situation.
- The golden rule respects the authority of Parliament because in all other circumstances the literal rule should be used.

Disadvantages of the golden rule
- As Michael Zander argues, it is 'a feeble parachute' because it allows judges to change the wording only when it is absurd or repugnant. It can therefore only be used in limited circumstances.
- As Zander also notes, it is 'an unpredictable safety valve' because there are no real guidelines on when it should be used. What seems to be absurd to one judge may not be absurd to another.
- As the Law Commission stated in 1969, the rule is of limited value and provides no clear means to test the existence of the characteristics of absurdity, inconsistency or inconvenience, or to measure their quality or extent.

The mischief rule

This rule was laid down in *Heydon's Case* (1584). Judges should consider four factors when using this rule:
  (1) What was the common law before the Act was passed?
  (2) What was the mischief that the Act was designed to remedy?
  (3) What was the remedy that Parliament was trying to provide?
  (4) What was the reason for the remedy?

Judges should look for the 'mischief' the Act was designed to remedy and interpret the Act in such a way that a remedy is achieved. This may mean disregarding the other rules.

This rule was used in *Smith* v *Hughes* (1960), where 'soliciting in the street' in the **Street Offences Act 1959** was held to include soliciting from the window of a house. The court said that the aim of the Act was to allow people to walk along the streets without being solicited, and it should be interpreted to cover this situation. In *Royal College of Nursing* v *DHSS* (1981), the court had to consider the wording of the Abortion Act 1967, which stated that pregnancies had to be terminated by a 'registered medical practitioner'. The House of Lords looked at the mischief that Parliament was aiming to redress — illegal, 'backstreet' abortions — and decided that having nurses (rather than doctors) supervising part of the abortion procedure was not unlawful. In *Elliott* v *Grey* (1959), a car was parked outside a house without a valid insurance policy; it had broken down some months before, the engine would not work and there was no petrol in the tank. The owner was convicted under s.35 of the **Road Traffic Act 1930** of using the car without valid insurance. Lord Chief Justice Parker in the divisional court said the mischief was the protection of third parties, so 'use' should be taken to mean 'have the use of'.

There are limitations on the use of the mischief rule. In *Jones* v *Wrotham Park* (1980), Lord Diplock said that it could only be used where:
- the mischief could be seen clearly from the Act
- it was apparent that Parliament had overlooked the problem
- additional words required could be stated with a high degree of certainty

Advantages of the mischief rule
- The mischief rule tries to give effect to the true intention of Parliament and so is regarded by most modern commentators as the best of the three rules.
- It allows judges, in Lord Denning's words, to 'fill in the gaps' when Parliament has left something out, and to use common sense and change wording in accordance with the problem that the Act was trying to deal with.
- It allows judges to interpret statutes in the light of changing social, economic and technological circumstances. A good example is the decision of the House of Lords in *Royal College of Nursing* v *DHSS* (1981), which recognised that medical practice had changed since the passing of the **Abortion Act 1967** because of the development of new techniques.
- It also allows the court to look at *Hansard*, so that the words of the minister bringing the bill before Parliament can be considered.
- As the Law Commission stated in 1969, it is a 'rather more satisfactory approach' than the other two rules.

Disadvantages of the mischief rule
- Finding the intention of Parliament is not easy, even if *Hansard* is used.
- The mischief rule could lead to confusion because judges could change the meaning of what an Act says. In *Stock* v *Frank Jones (Tipton) Ltd* (1978), Lord Simon argued that judges should think carefully before adding to the words of a statute, suggesting that sometimes leaving Parliament to legislate was 'far preferable to judicial contortion of the law to meet apparently hard cases with the result that ordinary citizens and their advisers hardly know where they stand'.

- It could be argued that it gives too much power to judges. Supporters of the literal rule, such as Viscount Simonds, would argue that Parliament should make any changes and that it would not be right for judges to try to second-guess what Parliament meant.

The purposive approach

The approach requires the court to examine the object of the Act and to construe doubtful passages in accordance with that purpose.

Over the last 20 years, the purposive approach has gained ground. The European Court of Justice uses this approach in interpreting EU law, and the English courts have to use the same approach when interpreting domestic legislation brought in as a result of this. The **Human Rights Act 1998** is also likely to cause a shift towards the purposive approach.

A good example of its use is *Jones* v *Tower Boot Co.* (1997), in which the Court of Appeal decided that racial harassment by fellow workers happened 'in the course of employment', making the employer liable. The Court of Appeal said that it was right to give the words a meaning other than their natural meaning so that the purpose of the legislation could be achieved.

Another example is *Coltman* v *Bibby Tankers* (1987), in which the House of Lords had to decide whether a ship, which had sunk, could be considered to be 'equipment' for the purposes of the **Employers' Liability (Defective Equipment) Act 1969**. Equipment was defined in the Act as including 'any plant and machinery, vehicle, aircraft and clothing', but the Law Lords decided that the purpose of the Act was clearly to protect workers in the workplace, and that as the ship had been defective in design and had caused death when it sank, it would be right to give the provision a broad construction.

Advantages of the purposive approach
- It fits in with what is done in Europe.
- It seems more sensible to look at the whole purpose of the Act rather than just at the evil it was designed to put right. This approach is wider than the other rules and allows judges to look at all the circumstances and consider the full range of evidence to find out what Parliament intended. In 1969, the Law Commission published a report called *The Interpretation of Statutes*. It favoured the use of the interpretation that best promoted the 'legislative purpose'. Similarly, Lord Denning, who was one of the greatest supporters of the purposive approach, argued in *Magor and St Melons* v *Newport Corporation* (1950) that the task for judges was to find out the intention of Parliament and to carry it out, and that this was best done by 'filling in the gaps and making sense of the enactments'.

Disadvantages of the purposive approach
- Some have argued that the purposive approach gives too much power to judges. For example, while Lord Denning contended that judges should look for the intention of Parliament, even when there is no ambiguity, Viscount Simonds described this approach as 'a naked usurpation of the legislative function under the thin disguise

of interpretation'. Lord Scarman also commented that 'if Parliament says one thing but means another, it is not...for the courts to correct it.... We are to be governed not by Parliament's intentions, but by Parliament's enactments'.

- Finding the intention of Parliament is not easy, even if *Hansard* is used. For example, in *R* v *Deegan* (1998) an application to consider *Hansard* was rejected because what ministers had said was not sufficiently clear.
- Using the purposive rule could lead to confusion because judges could change the meaning of what an Act says.

Rules of language

These are common-sense rules that have been developed over time. They allow the judges to look at other words in the Act in order to make the meaning of words and phrases clear. The rules are:

- ***ejusdem generis***: in a list, general words that follow specific words are limited to the same type as the specific ones. If an Act uses the phrase 'dogs, cats and other animals', the 'other animals' would include other domestic animals but not wild animals. This rule can be illustrated through the case of *Re Stockport Ragged, Industrial and Reformatory Schools* (1898), in which the courts had to consider the phrase 'cathedral, collegiate, chapter and other schools'. They decided that 'other schools' had to be limited to schools of the same kind as those in the list, which were all Church schools. The rule was also applied in *Powell* v *Kempton Park Racecourse* (1899), in which the court concluded that 'house, office, room or other place for betting' could not include open-air betting on the racecourse itself, because places specified in the list were all indoors.
- ***expressio unius est exclusio alterius***: express mention of one thing implies the exclusion of another. If an Act specifically referred to Labrador dogs, it would not include other breeds of dog. An example is *Tempest* v *Kilner* (1846), where a section of an Act included the words 'goods, wares and merchandise'. It was held that the section could not be taken to apply to stocks and shares, as they had not been included in the list.
- ***noscitur a sociis***: a word draws meaning from other words around it. Where an Act deals with houses 'for public refreshment, resort and entertainment', the last word is held not to cover theatrical or musical entertainment, but to refer to refreshment rooms and the reception and accommodation of the public. For example, in *Inland Revenue Commissioners* v *Frere* (1965), a section of an Act referred to 'interest, annuities or other annual interest'. Because of the reference 'other annual interest', the court decided that the first use of 'interest' must be restricted to annual interest (and therefore not apply to daily or monthly interest).

Conclusion

The courts are not told how to solve a particular problem. There is no indication, either in the 'rules' or elsewhere, as to which approach should be taken in any given situation.

In recent years, the courts have moved towards using the purposive approach and new extrinsic aids. However, the individual judge selects the method that he or she wishes to use when interpreting a statute. This could result in one judge using the literal approach, while another uses the purposive approach, with the two reaching opposite conclusions.

Judicial precedent

When the facts of a case are similar to a case that has already been decided, the judge must follow that previous decision, especially if it was reached by a higher court. This forms the basis of judicial precedent and is known as **stare decisis**, 'stand by the decision'.

The hierarchy of the courts

In order for the system of judicial precedent to work, there must be rules for judges to follow to make sure there is consistency in the law. One way of doing this is to have a hierarchy, so that decisions in the higher courts bind the lower courts. Some of the courts are also bound by their own previous decisions.

The European Court of Justice

Since the UK joined the European Community in 1973, decisions made by the European Court of Justice (ECJ) have been binding on all the courts in the UK in matters of EU law (e.g. the interpretation of treaties). The ECJ is not bound by its own previous decisions and can overrule them.

The House of Lords

The House of Lords is bound by the decisions of the ECJ, but as the highest appeal court in England, its decisions bind all the other English courts. Originally, except where a decision was made **per incuriam** ('in error'), the House of Lords was bound by its own previous decisions. This was established in *London Street Tramways* v *London County Council* (1898), in order to ensure certainty in the law. However, in 1966 the Lord Chancellor issued a **Practice Statement**, which stated:

> Their Lordships regard the use of precedent as an indispensable foundation upon which to decide what is the law and its application to individual cases. It provides at least some degree of certainty upon which individuals can rely in the conduct of their affairs, as well as a basis for the orderly development of legal rules. Their Lordships nevertheless recognise that too rigid adherence to precedent may lead to injustice in a particular case and also unduly restrict the proper development of the law. They propose therefore to modify their present practice and, while treating decisions of this house as normally binding, to depart from a decision when it appears right to do so.

This was seen as an important event, but in the years since that decision the House of Lords has used the power sparingly. The Lords has overruled its own previous decisions in the following cases:

- *British Railways Board* v *Herrington* (1972) overruled *Addie* v *Dumbreck* (1929) on the duty of care owed to a child trespasser.
- *Murphy* v *Brentwood District Council* (1990) overruled *Anns* v *Merton London Borough Council* (1977) on the duty of care owed by local authorities.
- *Pepper* v *Hart* (1993) overruled the House of Lords ruling in *Davis* v *Johnson* (1979) that banned the use of *Hansard* in statutory interpretation.
- *R* v *Shivpuri* (1986) overruled *Anderton* v *Ryan* (1985) on attempting the impossible in theft.
- *R* v *Howe* (1987) overruled *R* v *Lynch* (1975) and stated that duress was no defence to a murder charge.

The Court of Appeal

This court has two divisions, which deal solely with either civil cases or criminal cases. Both divisions are bound by decisions of the House of Lords and the ECJ, but the decisions of one division do not bind the other.

The Court of Appeal (Civil Division)

This division of the Court of Appeal is bound by its own previous decisions. The case of *Young* v *Bristol Aeroplane Co. Ltd* (1944) confirmed this, but set out three exceptions when the Civil Division can depart from its own previous decisions:

- The previous decision was made *per incuriam*, for example the decision was made without considering a relevant Act of Parliament.
- There are two Court of Appeal decisions that conflict.
- A later decision of the House of Lords overrules a previous decision in the Court of Appeal.

In the past, the Court of Appeal tried to argue that the Practice Statement should also apply to it, but in *Davis* v *Johnson* (1979) the House of Lords reaffirmed the rule in *Young*.

Note, however, that there are now two additional exceptions to the rule:

- It seems clear following s.3 of the **European Communities Act 1972** that the Court of Appeal can ignore a previous decision that is inconsistent with European Community law or a decision of the ECJ.
- Similarly, in s.2 of the **Human Rights Act 1998** the courts are bound to take into account judgements of the European Court of Human Rights, and presumably apply them rather than a previous Court of Appeal judgement.

The Court of Appeal (Criminal Division)

This division is usually bound by its own previous decisions but may take a more flexible approach if the liberty of an individual is involved. This was upheld in *R* v *Spencer* (1985). In *R* v *Simpson* (2003), a five-person Court of Appeal decided that it would overrule an earlier decision, not because the liberty of the defendant was at issue, but rather to ensure justice for the public at large and maintain confidence in the criminal justice system. The exceptions in *Young* also apply.

The High Court

The divisional courts and the ordinary High Court are all bound by the decisions of the Court of Appeal, the House of Lords and the ECJ. The Family Division and the Chancery Division (civil courts) are bound by their own previous decisions. There is more flexibility in the Queen's Bench Division when hearing appeals on criminal cases. The ordinary High Court is bound by the decisions of the divisional courts but not by its own previous decisions.

The Crown Court

This court is bound by the decisions of all the higher courts. Its decisions are not binding precedent, although the decisions of High Court judges sitting in the Crown Court could form persuasive precedent if reported. The court is not bound to follow its own decisions.

Magistrates' and County Courts

These courts are bound by the courts above them, but their own decisions do not form binding or persuasive precedent. They are not bound by their own previous decisions.

Ratio decidendi and binding precedent

When a judge, after hearing a case, presents his or her written judgement, this is known as **case law**. This judgement sets out the facts of the case and the legal principles that he or she has used to reach a decision. The legal principles are known as the ***ratio decidendi***, 'the reason for deciding'. This is the binding precedent for future cases where the facts are sufficiently similar and where the original case is decided in a court more senior (or, in some cases, at the same level) in the hierarchy. An example of *ratio decidendi* is the rule in *R* v *Nedrick* (1986), confirmed in *R* v *Woollin* (1997), that if a jury considers that the defendant foresaw death or serious injury as a virtual certainty, oblique intention may be inferred. Another example is the judgement in *R* v *Cunningham* (1957) that to be reckless you have to know there is a risk of an unlawful consequence and decide to take the risk.

Persuasive precedent

Obiter dicta statements

Sometimes the judge may speculate on what the decision might have been if the situation were different. This is known as ***obiter dicta***, 'things said by the way'. Although this is not part of the case law, it may influence judges in later cases as persuasive precedent. Lord Denning's *obiter dicta* statements in the case of *Central London Property Trust Ltd* v *High Trees House Ltd* (1947) led to the creation of the doctrine of **promissory estoppel**.

Another good example is in *Hall* v *Simons* (2000), which concerned allegedly negligent advice given by solicitors. Lord Hoffman's statement, that the rule giving advocates immunity for alleged negligence was no longer appropriate and should be abolished, is technically *obiter dicta*, but it has been treated as authoritative and will almost certainly be followed in future cases.

The comments by Lord Atkin in *Donoghue* v *Stevenson* (1932) are of a general nature and do not really go to the decision in the case. Therefore, they are almost certainly *obiter* comments rather than part of the *ratio*, and yet it is they rather than the reasons for the decision itself that have been accepted as providing the precedent for future cases.

Courts lower in the hierarchy

Persuasive precedent may also arise from the lower courts. The House of Lords agreed with the reasons that the Court of Appeal gave in the case of *R* v *R* (1991) when deciding that a man could be found guilty of raping his wife.

Dissenting judgements

When a court reaches a majority decision (in the Court of Appeal a case is usually heard by three judges, in the House of Lords by five), the dissenting judge(s) have to give their reasons for dissenting. If the case goes to appeal in a higher court, these reasons may be followed as persuasive precedent if the higher court disagrees with the majority decision of the lower court.

Decisions of the Judicial Committee of the Privy Council

Decisions of the Judicial Committee of the Privy Council (JCPC) are made as a result of its role as a court of final appeal for some Commonwealth countries (many of the judges in the court are members of the House of Lords and therefore very senior judges). These decisions are not binding on the English courts but they can also form persuasive precedent. The Court of Appeal in *Doughty* v *Turner Manufacturing Co. Ltd* (1964) chose to follow the JCPC decision, involving liability and remoteness of damage in the tort of negligence, in *The Wagon Mound No 1* (1961), rather than its own earlier decision in *Re Polemis* (1921).

The case of *Attorney General for Jersey* v *Holley* (2005) concerned the defence of provocation (the effect of which is to reduce murder to manslaughter); a nine-member Privy Council decided by six to three to follow an earlier Privy Council decision (in *Luc Thiet Thuan*, 1997) rather than the more recent House of Lords ruling (in *R* v *Smith*, 2000). The Court of Appeal in the cases of *R* v *James*, *R* v *Karami* (2006) has now confirmed that it will follow *Holley* rather than *Smith*.

Decisions in other countries

Sometimes the decisions of courts in the other Commonwealth countries, such as Canada, Australia and New Zealand, become persuasive precedent. For instance, in *Caparo* v *Dickman* (1990), the House of Lords approved a statement in an Australian case.

Law reporting

For the doctrine of judicial precedent to work properly there must be some way in which judges can find out if there are binding precedents in existence. This is achieved by an accurate record of law reporting. It is only since the development of modern law reporting in 1865 that systematic reporting has allowed the proper develoment of the system of precedent. Even today, there is no 'official set' of law reports, nor is there any official selection of the cases to be reported. The most authoritative set of reports are those produced by the Incorporated Council of Law Reporting (ICLR), set up for this purpose by the Law Society and the Inns of Court in 1865. They are known simply as 'The Law Reports' or as the 'Appeal Cases' (AC), and they report cases from the House of Lords, the Court of Appeal and the divisional courts of the High Court. A separate volume of *Weekly Law Reports* is also published by the ICLR. The *All England Law Reports* published by Butterworths appear weekly and may report cases which do not appear in the ICLR Law Reports. There are also specialised reports, such as the Family Law Reports or the Criminal Appeal Reports.

Many recent cases are now reported on the internet or on CD-ROMs and are often available within hours of the judgements being handed down. There are subscription services such as LexisNexis (the oldest of its kind) and Justis, and many case reports are available free.

How judges avoid following precedent

When deciding a case that appears to have a precedent, set either by the court hearing the case or a higher court, if the facts are similar the court must follow the precedent and apply the law in the same way. Judges can express their disapproval of a precedent that they feel obliged to follow, and this could be a signal either to Parliament or to a higher court that the law should be changed. There are, however, several approaches which judges can take in order to avoid following precedent.

Distinguishing

If the judge finds that the facts of a case are sufficiently different from the case setting the precedent, he or she can distinguish the two cases and avoid following precedent. In *King* v *Phillips* (1953), the Court of Appeal said that a mother who suffered shock after seeing her child's tricycle under a taxi and hearing the child scream was not owed a duty of care as the child was not injured in any way. In *Boardman* v *Sanderson* (1964), however, the claimaint's son was injured when the defendant negligently backed his car over him. The claimant was close by, heard the screams and suffered from shock; he was able to recover damages.

In *Balfour* v *Balfour* (1919), Mrs Balfour was unable to enforce a maintenance agreement made with her husband. The *ratio decidendi* of the case was that there is no intention to create legal relations when agreements are made within marriage. In *Merritt* v *Merritt* (1970), however, the defendant husband sought to rely on the Balfour principle to avoid honouring an agreement he had made with his estranged wife. The court distinguished the case on the material difference that the agreement, albeit made within marriage, had been made after the couple had separated, and the husband had to transfer the house to the wife as agreed. The decision limited the scope of the Balfour principle and created a new rule in respect of separated couples.

Overruling

Judges in the higher courts can overrule the decisions of the lower courts if they consider the legal principles to be wrong. As stated previously, the 1966 Practice Statement allows the House of Lords to depart from its own previous decisions, although it has rarely done so. An example is *Pepper* v *Hart* (1993), which overruled *Davis* v *Johnson* (1979) on the issue of whether *Hansard* could be referred to by judges interpreting statutes.

The Court of Appeal Civil Division also has the power to overrule its own earlier decisions, but only in the limited circumstances set out in *Young* v *Bristol Aeroplane Co. Ltd* (1944). The Criminal Division has rather more freedom. In *R* v *Simpson* (2003), it was able to overrule an earlier decision on the basis that justice needed to be achieved for the public at large and that confidence needed to be maintained in the criminal justice system.

Reversing

When a case goes to a higher court on appeal, the higher court may reverse the decision if it considers the law to be wrongly interpreted. A good example of this is the case of *Gillick* (1985). Mrs Gillick was a devout Catholic and mother of five daughters. She sought a declaration that her Area Health Authority's policy of allowing doctors to prescribe contraceptives to girls under 16 without parental consent was illegal. In the High Court, the case was decided against Mrs Gillick. She appealed, and the Court of Appeal reversed the decision. The Area Health Authority then appealed, and the House of Lords reversed the decision again.

Another example is *Sweet* v *Parsley* (1970). The defendant was convicted in the Magistrates' Court; her conviction was upheld in the divisional court and was then reversed by the House of Lords.

Advantages of precedent

Certainty and consistency

Certainty allows people to know what the law is, enabling lawyers to predict the likely outcome of a case. This may result in a case being settled out of court. Consistency occurs because similar cases are dealt with in the same way.

Flexibility

Flexibility arises through the use of overruling, distinguishing and reversing, allowing the law to evolve. Changes in attitude in society can be taken into account, an example being *R* v *R* (1991), when the House of Lords accepted that a man could be guilty of raping his wife.

Another example is *R* v *Malcherek and Steel* (1981), when the law was adapted to deal with the effect of life-support systems on judging what constitutes the exact point of death. The decision in *Malcherek* was that if the patient is already pronounced brain dead, switching off the life-support machine does not break the chain of causation between the initial injury and the death.

Precision

Precision arises because the statement of law always relates to the exact facts of the case, leading to detailed practical rules.

Disadvantages of precedent

Complexity and volume

The number of reported cases is large and growing continually. This makes it difficult to know all the cases that might be relevant. Judges may only be aware of those precedents that the parties concerned bring to their attention. There is also difficulty in determining the *ratio decidendi* of some reported cases because of the way in which the judgement is written.

Rigidity

The strict hierarchy means that judges have to follow binding precedent. Therefore, bad or inappropriate decisions cannot be changed unless they are heard in a higher court that can overrule them.

Unsystematic development

Due to the way case law operates, if a whole series of rules is based on one case, which is later overruled, this can cause problems.

Illogical distinctions

The use of distinguishing, in order to avoid precedent, has led to complexity in some areas of law. There may be only minute and apparently illogical differences between some cases. Too many distinctions of this type can lead to unpredictability.

Lack of democracy

When deciding cases in this way, judges are actually making law, which under the doctrine of the separation of powers is not part of their role.

Lack of research

In order to decide a case, a judge is only presented with the facts of the case and any legal arguments. Unlike Parliament, judges cannot commission research to assess the implications of their decisions.

Retrospective effect

Unlike legislation, which only applies to events after it has come into effect, case law applies retrospectively to events that occurred before the case was brought. This could lead to unfairness if as a result of the case the law is changed, because the parties to the case could not have known what the law was prior to their actions. This is what happened in *R* v *R* (1991), for example, the effect of which was to turn an act that was lawful at the time it was committed into a serious criminal offence.

The courts system

It is important that you understand the jurisdiction of the different courts in England and Wales — both civil and criminal — and the process of appeals to the Court of Appeal and the House of Lords.

Civil courts

Civil disputes involve individuals bringing claims against other individuals. Such claims can arise within the areas of contract, tort, land, employment and family law.

County Courts

There are more than 300 County Courts in England and Wales, which handle the majority of civil cases. They are situated in all large towns and cities, and their procedures are governed by the **County Courts Act 1984**. Trials are usually presided over by a circuit judge, although Recorders and district judges also sit in cases.

The jurisdiction of the County Court

The County Court has jurisdiction over a specific locality, within which defendants must live. If the defendant is a company, the registered office must be situated there.

All contract claims and almost all tort actions up to a value of £50,000 can be tried in the County Courts; the only tort action that cannot be tried is libel, which must be heard in the High Court. Most County Courts can deal with undefended divorce actions. Unless the legal issue in a family law case is particularly complicated, most of these cases are also dealt with by this court, especially probate (finalising the value of a deceased person's estate). The County Court can also hear bankruptcy cases, tax cases and land law disputes, most often those involving repossession orders sought by banks and building societies against home owners in arrears with mortgage payments. This area of law falls under the equitable jurisdiction of the court.

Note that under the Civil Procedure Rules (CPR), which implemented the Woolf Access to Justice recommendations, all fast-track actions must be taken in the County Court. Appeals are heard by a circuit judge (small claims cases), a single High Court judge (fast-track cases) or a Court of Appeal (multi-track cases). In all cases, leave to appeal must be granted.

Small claims arbitration procedure

Within the County Court is the small claims arbitration procedure, which currently has a jurisdiction to hear cases up to a value of £5,000 (£1,000 in personal injury cases). A district judge presides over this less formal procedure, where parties are usually unrepresented (as legal aid is not available) and costs are not awarded to the successful party. Most actions heard are for debt recovery and consumer problems. This arbitration has dealt with many cases that could not have been pursued in the County Court itself because of the high costs, delay and complexity. However, there have been problems over enforcement of court orders: about one third of successful claimants have been unable to recover their award of damages.

The High Court

The High Court is set up in divisions — Queen's Bench (QB), Chancery and Family — of which the Queen's Bench is the busiest, with over 70 High Court judges assigned to it. There is no financial limit to the jurisdiction of the High Court. While most cases are heard in London, the number of High Court sittings in other major cities is increasing.

Queen's Bench Division

The Queen's Bench Division traditionally hears contract and tort actions — it alone has jurisdiction to hear defamation (mainly libel) cases. Within this division are the Commercial Court and the Admiralty Court. The Queen's Bench is the most important of the divisional courts and has three main areas of jurisdiction:

(1) Under the **Magistrates' Courts Act 1980**, appeal to the Queen's Bench is 'by way of case stated' on a point of law. The Magistrates' Court sets out its findings of fact and the prosecution and defence cases, together with the legal rules applied, and then asks the Queen's Bench to determine the question of law in dispute.

(2) The most important and growing area of jurisdiction is that of judicial review, where two judges assess the legality or reasonableness of decisions/actions of public bodies, especially of government ministers.

(3) The Queen's Bench has general oversight of all inferior courts, tribunals and any body exercising a quasi-judicial function. It regulates this jurisdiction by prerogative orders of *certiorari* (order directing that a record of proceedings in a lower court be sent up for review), prohibition (order forbidding an inferior court to determine a matter outside its jurisdiction) and *mandamus* (order commanding an inferior tribunal, public official, corporation etc. to carry out a public duty).

Chancery Division

The Chancery Division mainly exercises an equitable jurisdiction and deals with contested probate matters, trusts, mortgages, bankruptcies, company and partnership cases, and taxation matters.

Family Division

This court has jurisdiction over matrimonial matters, including contested divorce actions, wardship, adoption and uncontested probate matters. Note that some of the most difficult legal cases, such as *Bland* v *Airedale NHS Trust* (1993) and *Re A (Conjoined Twins)* (2000), come before this court.

The Court of Appeal (Civil Division)

Most appeals to this court come from the High Court, but it may also hear appeals from multi-track actions in the County Court. Although most appeals involve questions of law, the court will also hear appeals over the amount of damages awarded, e.g. in libel cases (see the case of *Sutcliffe* v *Pressdram*, 1990). Leave to appeal must be granted either by the lower court or by the Court of Appeal itself. After the hearing, the Appeal Court can reverse or uphold the lower court's decision, vary the award or (rarely) order a retrial.

The House of Lords

Unlike all other courts described above, the House of Lords, when hearing civil cases, sits as a UK court, as it takes civil appeals from both Scotland and Northern Ireland. It only hears approximately 60 cases a year, mostly civil, many of which concern tax law. The majority of appeals come from the Court of Appeal or the Scottish Court of Session, but it is possible for cases to come directly to the House of Lords from the High Court using the 'leap-frog' procedure, though this is rare.

Leave to appeal to the House of Lords must be given either by the lower court, usually the Court of Appeal, or by two Law Lords, where such leave has not been granted. Only cases that raise a point of law of general public importance will be heard here.

Disadvantages of civil courts

Too expensive

Research carried out for Lord Woolf's review found that one side's costs exceeded the amount in dispute in over 40% of claims for under £12,500. Where the claim was for between £12,500 and £25,000, average costs were between 40% and 95% of the claim. The bill for one claim of just £2,000 came to £69,295. The survey concluded that the simplest cases often incurred the highest costs in proportion to the value of the claim (see *Campbell* v *MGN*, 2004).

Because of the complexity of the civil courts procedure, lawyers are usually needed. High Court litigation is not for the inexperienced, so barristers draft the pleadings and advise on the evidence. To employ such legal expertise is expensive. The sheer length of civil proceedings also impacts on the costs.

Delays

The Civil Justice Review, set up in 1985, observed that the system was overstretched, and that the time between the incident that gave rise to the claim and the trial could be up to 3 years for County Courts and 5 years for the High Court. Research carried out for Lord Woolf found that the worst delays were in personal injury and medical negligence cases, which took a median time of 54 and 61 months respectively. The average waiting time for a County Court claim was 79 weeks. Although time limits were laid down for each stage of the action, both judges and lawyers disregarded them. Often, lawyers waived time limits in order to create an opportunity to negotiate; this was reasonable, but there was no effective control of when and why it was done.

According to the 1985 review, long delays placed intolerable psychological and financial burdens on accident victims. They also undermined the justice of the trial by making it more difficult to gather evidence; this evidence was then unreliable because witnesses had to remember the events of several years before. The overall result was to lower public esteem of the legal system.

Injustice

Usually, an out-of-court settlement is negotiated before the litigants ever reach trial. For every 9,000 personal injury cases commenced, only 300 reach trial. Outside such cases, for every 100,000 writs issued before 1999, fewer than 300 came to trial. There are advantages to reaching such a settlement — a quick end to the dispute and a significant reduction in costs — but it can equally be argued that the high number of such settlements creates injustice because the parties often hold unequal bargaining positions.

Finally, the rules on payments in court increase the unfairness of the pre-trial procedures. As Professor Zander observed, the rule is 'highly favourable' to the defendant, and puts pressure on the claimant to accept an offer.

The adversarial process

Many problems result from the adversarial process, which encourages tactical manoeuvring rather than cooperation. It would be far simpler, and therefore cheaper, for each side to state precisely what it alleges in the pleadings, disclose all the documents it holds, and give the other side copies of its witness statements. Note that before the Civil Procedure Rules were introduced, there was almost a complete lack of judicial trial management.

Advantages of civil courts

While most students are able to state the problems of civil courts in terms of delay, expense and formality, comparatively few can explain the advantages that these courts have over any other form of dispute resolution.

Compulsory process

There is no other process by which you can effectively compel the other side to come to a forum to resolve a dispute. The other party could, of course, decline to lodge a defence or even to appear in court, but in that case, a default judgement would be issued against it.

Formality of procedures

Rules of evidence, disclosure and legal argument all ensure a fair process. This process is supervised by a judge, who is a trained and qualified expert in the law and legal processes.

Appeal process

No other dispute-resolution process allows for appeals. In many tribunals, there is no appellate tribunal, and an appeal to the Queen's Bench Divisional Court is only allowed on a point of law. This is also the position with arbitration. Such appeals are rare.

Legal aid

Although civil legal aid has been greatly reduced in recent years, particularly as a result of reforms in the **Access to Justice Act 1999**, it is still more widely available for court litigation than for any alternative. It is also true that lawyers are more likely to litigate on a conditional fee basis in court than in tribunals, arbitration or mediation.

Law making and development

Only courts, especially the Court of Appeal and the House of Lords, can make and develop legal rules through the doctrine of precedent. Any decision given in arbitration, and even in tribunals, applies only to the case in question. It is essential, in the areas of business and taxation, for companies and individuals to understand the relevant legal rules, and to be able to challenge these through the appellate system to allow the law to develop.

Enforcement of decision

Courts have greater powers to enforce their decisions than any other dispute-resolution agency.

The civil justice system after April 1999

On 26 April 1999, new Civil Procedure Rules (CPR) came into force. They constitute a fundamental reform of the civil justice system, introducing the main recommendations of Lord Woolf. He described the rules as providing 'a new landscape for civil justice for the twenty-first century'.

The reformed rules aim to eliminate unnecessary cost, delay and complexity. The general approach of Lord Woolf is reflected in his statement: 'If "time and money are no object" was the right approach in the past, it certainly is not today.'

The first rule of the CPR sets the overriding objective of the whole system — that the rules should enable the courts to deal with cases 'justly'. This objective prevails over all other rules in the case of a conflict. The parties and their lawyers are now expected to assist the judges in achieving this objective.

Dealing with a case 'justly' involves the following factors:
- ensuring the parties are on an equal footing
- saving expense
- ensuring 'proportionality' in the way the case is dealt with in terms of the value of the claim, the importance and complexity of the case and the financial position of each party
- ensuring that it is dealt with expeditiously and fairly
- allotting to it an appropriate share of the court's resources

The emphasis of the new rules is on avoiding litigation by means of pre-trial settlements. Litigation is to be viewed as a last resort; the court has a continuing obligation to encourage and facilitate settlement. As pre-trial procedures are the most important area of the civil process because so few cases actually come to trial, Lord Woolf recommended the development of **pre-action protocols** to lay down a code of conduct for this stage of the proceedings. These aim to encourage:
- more pre-action contact between the parties
- an earlier and more comprehensive exchange of information
- improved pre-action investigation
- a settlement before trial proceedings have commenced

Through establishing a timetable for the exchange of information etc., the parties are better informed as to the merits of their case and so are in a position to settle cases fairly, which reduces the need for litigation. If they cannot settle, the parties should be able to go to trial on a more informed basis and thus ensure that the trial itself can run to a tighter timetable.

Alternative dispute resolution (ADR)

This is greatly encouraged and actively promoted by the court. There is a general state-ment in the Civil Procedure Rules that the court's duty to further the overriding objec-tive by active case management includes both encouraging the parties to use an ADR procedure and facilitating the use of that procedure.

An excellent example of the 'pressure' to make ADR successful was provided by the case of *Dunnett* v *Railtrack plc* (2002). Railtrack, which won the case, was not awarded its costs because it had 'turned down flat' an offer of ADR after the court had sug-gested that this would be the best way to resolve the dispute between the parties. As the claim by Mrs Dunnett was only for £9,000 and the legal costs of taking the case up to the Court of Appeal amounted to more than £100,000, Railtrack made an expensive mistake.

Recently, the Court of Appeal has delivered important guidance on the use of mediation and ADR in personal injury litigation. In the consolidated appeals of *Halsey* v *Milton Keynes General NHS Trust* and *Steel* v *Joy and Halliday* (2004), the court ruled on when it is appropriate to penalise a party who refuses mediation.

The *Halsey* case was a clinical negligence claim involving an elderly patient. Invitations to mediate were made by the claimant but refused because the defendant argued that the claim had no prospect of success and the nominal value of the claim meant the cost of mediation would be disproportionate. The claim was dismissed and the judge refused to penalise the Trust for its failure to mediate.

In the *Steel* case, a personal injury claim was brought following two accidents. The defendant to the first accident had offered to mediate, but the defendant to the second had refused because it felt the case was strong and refused to compromise. The Court of Appeal found that this was reasonable.

The court took the opportunity to issue some guidelines for the use of mediation and ADR in personal injury cases, which included the following:
- The court does not have the power to order reluctant litigants to mediate, and to do so would infringe human rights legislation.
- The court's role is to encourage but not compel parties to enter into mediation.
- Where a party reasonably believes that its case is 'water-tight', e.g. where it would have succeeded on a summary judgement application, it may be justified in refusing mediation.

- The court should consider whether the costs of mediation would be disproportionately high.
- All those involved in litigation should routinely consider with their clients whether their disputes are suitable for ADR.
- If the successful party acted unreasonably in refusing ADR, the court can displace the normal costs rule and order that party to pay costs, despite its winning at trial.
- The burden of showing that the refusing party was acting unreasonably lies with the unsuccessful party.

Case management

This is the most significant innovation of the 1999 reforms: the court is the active manager of the litigation. Traditionally, the parties and their lawyers were left to manage their cases. However, the new rules aim to bring cases to trial quickly and efficiently, placing the management of cases in the hands of the judges and emphasising the court's duty to take a proactive role in the administration of each case.

Once proceedings have commenced, the court's powers of case management are triggered by the filing of a defence and/or counterclaim. The court first needs to allocate the case to one of three tracks, which determines the future conduct of the proceedings:
- **small claims** — actions under £5,000
- **fast-track** — actions between £5,000 and £15,000
- **multi-track** — actions over £15,000

Small claims
There is no significant change to previous procedures apart from increased jurisdiction to £5,000. (Its previous jurisdictional limit was £3,000.)

Fast-track
These cases are normally dealt with in the County Court. The court gives directions for the management of the case and sets a timetable for the disclosure, the exchange of witness statements, the exchange of expert witnesses and the trial date, or the period within which the trial will take place, which will be no more than 30 weeks later. (Before 1999, trials took place, on average, 80 weeks later.)

In an attempt to limit legal expenses, fixed costs have been recommended for fast-track trials, although these have not yet been introduced. Lord Woolf recommended that there should be a £2,500 limit on costs for fast-track cases.

Multi-track
The court can give directions for the management of a multi-track case and can set a timetable for the steps to be taken. Alternatively, for more serious cases, the court may fix a case management conference or a pre-trial review or both. The court does not at this stage automatically set a trial date or a period within which the trial will take place.

Criminal courts

Classification of offences

There are three different classes of criminal offence:

- **summary** — minor offences that can only be tried by Magistrates' Courts, e.g. motoring offences
- **either-way** — offences that may be tried either by magistrates or in a Crown Court before a judge and jury, e.g. theft
- **indictable** — serious offences that can only be tried in a Crown Court before a judge and jury, e.g. murder

The Magistrates' Court

The Magistrates' Court is the 'workhorse of the criminal justice system' and is responsible for hearing over 1 million cases each year. All summary offences and the majority of either-way offences are tried by Magistrates' Courts. Within these courts are the youth courts, which have the jurisdiction to try all offences charged against those aged from 10 to 17 (excluding murder, which can only be tried in a Crown Court).

Appeals are made to the Queen's Bench Division of the High Court on a point of law by way of case stated, or to the Crown Court against sentence or conviction.

The Crown Court

Although the Crown Court acts as an appeal court, hearing cases from Magistrates' Courts, its main jurisdiction is to hear all indictable offences (such as murder, rape and robbery) and the more serious either-way offences, where jurisdiction has been declined by magistrates or where the defendant has elected to be tried on indictment by a judge sitting with a jury.

Cases are tried by different judges, depending on the seriousness of the offence:

- All Class 1 offences (murder) must be tried by a High Court judge from the Queen's Bench Division. Such judges also try the majority of Class 2 offences — those offences that can result in a life sentence (e.g. rape, robbery and attempted murder).
- Other less serious offences are tried by circuit judges or Recorders. In all cases heard in Crown Courts, the decision on the defendant's guilt or innocence is taken by the jury.

The Court of Appeal (Criminal Division)

This is presided over by the Lord Chief Justice. Three judges make up the panel that hears appeals, usually a Lord Justice of Appeal accompanied by two senior High Court judges from the Queen's Bench Division. In more important appeals, all the judges will be Lord Justices.

Appeals may be made to this court by defendants against sentence or conviction from the Crown Court, provided leave to appeal has been granted. In appeals against sentence, the Court of Appeal may confirm or reduce the sentence imposed at trial. Additionally, the court may lay down or vary a 'tariff' sentence: this is where the Court of Appeal establishes a clear guideline on sentencing for a particular offence to assist trial judges.

The principal grounds for appealing against conviction are that the original conviction is 'unsafe or unsatisfactory', new evidence not available at the time of trial has come to light, or there has been a material irregularity in the course of the trial. The court can uphold the original conviction, quash it (i.e. overturn it and release the defendant), substitute a lower-level conviction (e.g. a manslaughter conviction where the original conviction was for murder) or order a retrial.

Appeals by the Attorney General

Under s.35 of the **Criminal Justice Act 1988**, the Attorney General, acting on behalf of the Crown Prosecution Service, can, with the leave of the court, appeal to the Court of Appeal against 'an unduly lenient sentence'.

The Attorney General can also refer a case to the Court of Appeal following an acquittal in the Crown Court, which he or she has reason to believe was the result of an error in law made by the judge in his or her directions to the jury. The purpose of such a referral is to verify the correct legal rule. The defendant, having been acquitted, is not identified in the citation, which is simply listed as 'Attorney General's Reference No... of [year]', and whatever decision on the law is made by the Court of Appeal, the acquittal is not affected in any way.

Criminal Cases Review Commission

This independent commission, established under the **Criminal Appeal Act 1995** and presided over by a lay person, has taken over the powers previously exercised by the Home Office to investigate alleged miscarriages of justice, which had been so heavily criticised by the Runciman Royal Commission on Criminal Justice. The commission 'must consider that there is a "real possibility" that the conviction, verdict, finding or sentence would not be upheld were the reference to be made'. An example of such a reference is the case of Sally Clarke (2003), whose conviction for the murders of her two children was quashed following the disclosure that forensic evidence was flawed.

Alternatives to courts

Tribunals

The past century has seen considerable growth in the potential for disputes between individuals, groups and state agencies. The expansion of agencies created for the implementation of state interventionist policies, as in the field of welfare provision, has created, in turn, the potential for disputes between individuals and social welfare officials, and between property owners and planning authorities. Frequently, the legislation that established the machinery for implementing such policies has also set up the institutional framework within which disputes in particular fields are to be resolved. It is significant that in many such cases, the dispute-solving mechanisms adopted have not been ordinary courts of law, but rather specialised tribunals.

If all disputes created under the weight of social legislation had to be settled in ordinary courts, the court system would collapse under the enormous workload. Furthermore, the courts are, for many of these cases, inappropriate for dealing with the dispute. For example, it would be completely out of place for a County Court to hear a social security claim for a few pounds a week, where the usual delays affecting court cases would operate harshly on the claimant who needs an immediate decision.

In order to provide a system for resolving disputes without the trappings of law courts, various governments have introduced, through legislation, a network of administrative tribunals designed to provide instant justice cheaply, efficiently and with minimum delay and formality. These tribunals comprise not highly paid judges but panels made up of a chairperson, who is usually legally qualified, and two non-legally qualified people who have expertise in the particular field over which the tribunal has jurisdiction. In all, there are about 70 different types of tribunal, hearing over 1 million cases each year. In England and Wales, more people take cases to tribunals than to any other part of the justice system.

Because tribunals have been set up by different statutes over a period of time, the problem of diversity between different types of tribunal was one of the key issues addressed by the Franks Committee, which reported its recommendations in 1957. The result was the **Tribunals and Inquiries Act 1958**, whose provisions are now contained in the **Tribunals and Inquiries Act 1992**. While this diversity has led to a confusing network of tribunals dealing with different areas and incorporating different procedures, it must be remembered that tribunals are *specialised* bodies, dealing with limited areas, and that this specialisation must be contrasted with courts of law, which have a much wider jurisdiction and hear many kinds of disputes involving different fields of law.

The Franks Committee recommended that tribunal procedures should be characterised by 'openness, fairness and impartiality':
- **Openness** requires, where possible, hearings to take place in public and reasons for decisions to be given.
- **Fairness** entails the adoption of clear procedures that allow parties to know their rights, present their case fully and be aware of the case against them.
- **Impartiality** means that tribunals should be free of undue influence from any government departments concerned with their subject area.

The committee was particularly concerned that tribunals were on ministry premises, with ministry staff presiding.

The committee also recommended the establishment of two permanent councils on tribunals to supervise procedures, one for England and Wales, and one for Scotland. Although a council was set up (with a Scottish committee), its functions are only advisory — it has little real power, and cannot reverse or even direct further consideration of individual tribunal decisions.

Advantages of tribunals

Speed
Tribunal cases come to court quickly and are often dealt with in a day. It is usually possible to specify the exact date and time when a case will be heard, thus minimising time wasting for the parties. In some tribunals, e.g. employment tribunals, it is common for a process of mediation or conciliation to be used to deal with the case initially. This often results in a solution without the need for a full hearing, which in turn saves further time and expense.

Cost
Tribunals do not usually charge fees, with each party paying its own costs, rather than the loser having to pay everything. The simpler procedures of tribunals mean that legal representation is unnecessary, and costs are therefore reduced.

Informality
The level or formality varies between different tribunals, but, as a general rule, wigs are not worn, the strict rules of evidence do not apply and attempts are made to create an unintimidating atmosphere. This is important when individuals are representing themselves.

Flexibility
Although tribunals aim to apply principles consistently, they do not operate strict rules of precedent and are therefore able to respond more flexibly than courts. Few of their decisions are reported formally.

Specialisation
Tribunal members already have expertise in the relevant subject area, and through sitting on tribunals they are able to build up a depth of knowledge that judges in ordinary courts could not hope to match.

Reduces pressure on courts
Without tribunals, ordinary courts would be swamped with cases, and delays would be many times worse than they are at present.

Awareness of policy
Because of their expertise, tribunal members are likely to understand the policy behind legislation. They often have wide, discretionary powers, which allow them to put policy into practice.

Privacy
Tribunals may, in some circumstances, meet in private, so that individuals are not obliged to have their problems aired in public.

Disadvantages of tribunals

Lack of openness

The fact that some tribunals are held in private can lead to suspicion about the fairness of their decisions.

Unavailability of legal aid

Full civil legal aid is available for only three tribunals — prison disciplinary, mental health and the parole board. Although assistance in case preparation is available under the legal advice and assistance scheme, this does not cover representation.

Tribunals are designed to obviate the need for legal representation, but in many cases the ordinary claimant faces an opponent with access to the best representation, e.g. an employer or a government department, and this places him or her at a serious disadvantage. Even though the procedures are generally informal compared with litigation, the average person is likely to be out of his or her depth. Research by Genn and Genn in 1989 found that much of the law with which tribunals are concerned is complex, and adjudication processes are sometimes highly technical. The Free Representation Unit (FRU) statistics indicate that individuals who are represented have a better chance of winning their cases.

There is, however, some dispute about the desirability of such representation involving lawyers. Although in certain cases this is the most appropriate form of representation, there are fears that the introduction of lawyers could affect the aims of speed and informality. If money for tribunal representation were available, it might be better spent on developing lay representation, such as that offered by specialist agencies, e.g. the UK Immigration Advisory Service or the Child Poverty Action Group, which can develop real expertise in specific areas, as well as general agencies such as Citizens Advice Bureaux. However, there is no real likelihood of any additional funding being made available by governments.

Lack of independence

The requirement of independence defined by Franks is compromised by the fact that members of some tribunals are appointed by the minister on whose decisions they have to adjudicate. Although there is no evidence that this results in bias, it is difficult for such tribunals to achieve the appearance of impartiality.

Lack of reasons

Reasons for decisions are not always given, although this has been strongly recommended by the Court of Appeal and is a requirement of the **Human Rights Act 1998**.

Too complex

The 1979 Royal Commission on Legal Services (the Benson Commission) recommended a review of tribunal procedures, with a view to simplifying the process so that applicants could as far as possible represent themselves. However, if anything, tribunal procedures have become more legalistic. The research of Genn and Genn appears to confirm that self-representation is difficult before some tribunals and therefore better legal or lay representation will become more necessary.

Lack of accessibility

The recommendation of the Franks Report that tribunals should be 'open' requires more than issuing a rule that hearings should usually be held in public; it also demands that citizens should be aware of tribunals and their right to use them. In cases where the dispute is between a citizen and the government, the citizen will usually be notified of procedures to be followed, but in other cases more thought needs to be given to publicising citizens' rights.

Problems with control

Considered together, tribunals vary widely and make thousands of decisions each year in different types of case. It is not easy to supervise this diversity. Indeed, the Council on Tribunals is only advisory/consultative.

Appeals

Sir Andrew Leggatt in his comprehensive report on tribunals stated that:

> There is a confusing variety of routes of appeal from tribunal decisions. The system has been rightly described as a hotch-potch. While it is important that there should be effective rights of appeal, in some tribunals there are too many stages, leading to long delays in reaching finality. There should be a right of appeal on a point of law, by permission, on the generic ground that the decision of the tribunal was unlawful:
> - from the first-tier tribunals in each Division to its corresponding appellate tribunal
> - from appellate tribunals to the Court of Appeal
> - where there is no corresponding appellate tribunal, to any such court as may be prescribed by statute

To address these issues, under the **Tribunals, Courts and Enforcement Act 2007** tribunals were brought together into a single system within the Justice Department and are administered by the Tribunals Service. The Act has also created a new system of upper tribunals to unify appellate and review functions for specified cases.

Non-adversarial procedures

There have been recent developments in the UK to encourage the use of non-adversarial procedures in the settlement of disputes, including mediation, conciliation and mini-trials. The most formal type of alternative dispute resolution (ADR) is arbitration.

ADR schemes have been in use in the USA, Australia, Canada and New Zealand for many years, and have been endorsed by the current Lord Chancellor in the light of major criticisms of the civil justice system and the pressures on legal aid. A court decision offers certainty and finality (subject to rights of appeal), but such decisions are often outweighed by delay, cost and the stress of undertaking litigation.

ADR attempts to involve the client in the process of resolving the dispute. It does not rely on an adversarial approach but rather on reaching an agreement. Each case is decided on its merits without reference to previous cases, and the common ground between the parties should be emphasised, rather than focusing on points of disagreement. ADR offers a confidential process, and the outcome will not be published without the consent of both parties. Resolution of a dispute can be fast and straightforward, and hearing times and places are at the agreement of both parties.

Arbitration

Arbitration may be defined as the determination of a dispute by an impartial person (rather than a court) after hearing both sides in a judicial manner. It is an increasingly popular way of resolving disputes, where both parties voluntarily agree to an independent third party making a decision in their case. It has been described as 'privatised litigation with the judge and venue paid for by the parties'. The process is governed by the **Arbitration Act 1996**.

The arbitrator is usually chosen by the parties and may be a businessperson or lawyer or someone with technical knowledge, e.g. an engineer or architect, according to the basis of the dispute. The date, place and time, the method of arbitration and the powers of the arbitrator are all matters for the parties to decide in consultation with the arbitrator.

There are different types of arbitration:

- **Small claims court**. Although the small claims court takes place as part of the jurisdiction of the County Court, the procedure followed is that of arbitration. The district judge is not bound to adopt strict court rules of evidence and procedure, and acts in effect as an arbitrator. The financial limit is £5,000 and most cases involve debt recovery or consumer problems.
- **Consumer arbitration**. The Office of Fair Trading (OFT) has in recent years encouraged and approved many arbitration schemes set up by trade associations to resolve consumer problems, e.g. the Association of British Travel Agents (ABTA). Usually, these involve a 'paper' arbitration, where the arbitrator makes the decision after reading the documents of the case, although it may be possible for there to be a hearing where the parties give evidence.
- **Commercial arbitration**. The complexity of business contracts makes disputes likely. One way to limit the damage and expense caused by such disputes is for the parties to go to arbitration rather than to the courts. Arbitration is more likely to maintain business relations between the parties than the more adversarial court process. For these reasons, many business contracts contain a *Scott* v *Avery* clause, whereby disputes must first be referred to arbitration. In such cases, it is likely that the arbitrator will be a member or fellow of the Institute of Arbitrators and as such will have legal knowledge of the matter in dispute. Note that the Commercial Court (part of the Queen's Bench Division) can, at the request of both parties, adjourn the court litigation and instead decide the issue by arbitration.

Advantages of arbitration

- Parties retain more control over arbitration than over a court case, where the control is effectively exercised by lawyers and the judge.
- The proceedings are held in private — an important consideration for commercial disputes.
- Arbitration is usually quicker and cheaper than court proceedings.

- In addition to having legal knowledge of the issue in dispute, an arbitrator will also be an expert in that area.

Disadvantages of arbitration

- There is no legal aid available.
- Opportunity to appeal is limited.
- There may be difficulty in enforcing awards.
- There may be an imbalance between parties, e.g. consumer against company.

Mediation

Mediation is an informal procedure that assists disputing parties in their negotiations. It involves an independent, neutral third party acting as a go-between to facilitate cooperation and agreement. The mediator will often discuss the disputed matter with each party in separate rooms. Where the relationship between the parties needs to be preserved, as in family disputes or those involving commercial matters, mediation ensures that the relationship is not soured as it would be by litigation. Mediation is a voluntary process and, should it fail, the parties will have preserved their positions. It also allows the parties to feel in control.

Mediation is widely used in the USA in family and corporate disputes. It can also be used to settle priorities before the start of litigation or, in some cases, in place of litigation. However, its use presupposes a degree of cooperation between the parties, and where parties are entrenched, mediation is inappropriate.

In the UK, commercial mediation is promoted and organised by companies such as International Resolution Europe Ltd and the Centre for Dispute Resolution, founded in 1990 under the auspices of the Confederation of British Industry. Mediation in family disputes is available from the National Association of Family Mediation and Conciliation Services, which offers support to those who wish to conduct their own negotiations and only refer to lawyers in an advisory capacity. Some 300 mediators throughout the UK offer family counselling and legal advice; they are trained solicitors and counsellors, whose aim is to arrive at mutually agreed settlements. Note the importance attached to mediation in the **Family Law Act 1996**, which aims to take divorce settlements out of the courts and establish family mediation centres throughout the UK.

Conciliation

Conciliation falls somewhere between arbitration and mediation, the former being the most formal, the latter the least formal. The conciliator offers a non-binding opinion, which may lead to a settlement.

Conciliation is widely used in the USA to settle commercial disputes. Lawyers representing each side present the arguments in the case to the parties and a neutral adviser, who may be a judge or senior lawyer. This enables the parties to assess the strengths, weaknesses and prospects of the case and gives them the opportunity to enter into settlement discussions on a realistic, business-like basis.

Conclusion

The aim of ADR is to facilitate settlement, whereas the aim of litigation is to obtain judgement, but note that judges are increasingly becoming involved with ADR, and barristers and solicitors too. In 1993, a Practice Statement issued by the Commercial Court (of the Queen's Bench Division) stated that parties should be encouraged to consider using ADR as an additional means of settling disputes. Judges of the Commercial Court can offer arbitration but not mediation or conciliation, although the clerk to the court retains a list of bodies offering such services.

The Committee on Alternative Dispute Resolution, established by the Bar Council and chaired by Lord Justice Beldam, published its report in 1991 that advocated courts embracing ADR in order to support the judicial process. Consequently, potential litigants or their legal representatives should undertake such procedures before resorting to litigation.

In his Access to Justice report, Lord Woolf recommended greater use of ADR, for example the use of neutral experts to assist in reaching a pre-trial settlement, independent mediation, or a separate tribunal or specialist arbitration scheme in small claims involving medical negligence.

Lay people

Juries

The jury system was imported into Britain after the Norman conquest, though its early functions were quite different from those it fulfils today. The first jurors acted as witnesses, providing information about local matters. Under Henry II, jurors began to take on an important judicial function, moving from reporting on events they knew about to deliberating on evidence produced by the parties involved in a dispute.

A major milestone in the history of the jury was *Bushell's Case* (1670), where it was finally established that the jury members were the sole judges of fact, had the right to give a verdict according to their conscience and could not be penalised for taking a view of the facts opposed to that of the judge. The importance of this power now is that a jury may acquit a defendant, even when the law demands a guilty verdict.

Juries, although important in our system of criminal justice, take part in fewer than 1% of all criminal trials — over 96% of criminal trials are conducted in Magistrates' Courts, and approximately 70% of defendants in Crown Courts plead guilty. A further proportion of defendants are found not guilty by means of 'directed acquittals', where the trial judge instructs the jury as a matter of law to return a formal verdict of 'not guilty'. In civil cases, juries are only involved in about 12 cases a year, mostly libel cases in the High Court.

Selection of jurors

Before 1972, only people who owned a home over a certain rateable value were eligible for jury service. The Morris Committee in 1965 estimated that 78% of those on the electoral register did not qualify for jury service, and 95% of women were ineligible. The current qualifications for jury service are detailed in the **Juries Act 1974**, which provides that potential jury members must be:

- aged between 18 and 70 years
- on the electoral register
- resident in the UK, Channel Islands or Isle of Man for at least 5 years since the age of 13

The jury summoning officer arranges for potential jurors' names to be picked at random from the electoral register by the Central Jury Summoning Bureau. From those selected (who are not excused or do not have jury service deferred), 20 are chosen randomly by the jury usher for the particular trial. These potential jurors — the 'jury in waiting' — are then told the name of the defendant and asked if they know him or her. If they do, they leave the court and return to the jury pool to be used for another trial. At court, a final random selection takes place and 12 jurors are selected to form a jury. However, some people are either excluded or excused from jury service on the following grounds:

- **Disqualification** — those with a criminal conviction who have received a custodial or community sentence within the last 10 years are disqualified. Imprisonment for 5 years or more results in life-time disqualification. Offenders on bail are also disqualified.
- **Ineligibility** — under the **Criminal Justice Act 2003**, which came into operation in 2004, the only people ineligible for jury service are those suffering from a mental illness who are resident in a hospital or have regular treatment by a medical practitioner.
- **Excusal as of right** — with the exception of those aged between 65 and 70, this category was abolished by the **Criminal Justice Act 2003**. This change has the effect of enabling clergymen, lawyers, police officers and even judges to become jurors.
- **Excusal at the court's discretion** — those with limited understanding of English, students doing public examinations, parents with childcare commitments/problems or people with prior commitments such as booked holidays may be excused from jury service. However, in such cases it is more likely that jury service will be deferred rather than cancelled. Full-time members of the armed forces may be excused if their commanding officer certifies that their absence from duty would be prejudicial to the efficiency of the service.

R v Abdroikov; R v Green; R v Williamson (2007)

This specific problem — that of lawyers, judges and police officers being eligible for jury service — formed the basis of an important appeal against conviction to the House of Lords. Three separate cases were heard together. In the first, there was a police officer on the jury where police evidence was not in issue. In the second, the crime victim was a police officer and the officer on the jury was from the same local police background (although he did not know the victim). In the third case, an experienced Crown Prosecution Service prosecutor was allowed by the judge to sit on the jury trying a serious rape case.

The House of Lords was anxious to emphasise that there was no evidence of any actual bias in any of these cases. However, as Lord Bingham explained, the principle was not only that justice must be done 'but should manifestly and undoubtedly be seen to be done'. Most adult human beings, he said, harbour certain prejudices and predilections because of their background, education and experience, but the court system does its best to neutralise the effect of these, not least by insisting that at least ten jurors should agree on a person's guilt. Nonetheless, Lord Bingham and a majority of the court held that in the police victim case and the CPS prosecutor case, a reasonable onlooker would conclude that justice had not been seen to be done because of the proximity of the jurors to the issues to be decided. These convictions were quashed — although in the serious rape case there may be a retrial.

Adapted from an article by Stephen Cragg, *The Times*, 23 October 2007

Jury challenging and vetting

In the UK, challenging a juror is a rare event, but there are three main ways in which it can occur:

(1) Prosecution can use '**Stand by for the Crown**' without giving a reason, although the Attorney General announced in 1988 that this right would only be used to remove a 'manifestly unsuitable' juror or to remove a juror in a terrorist/security trial where jury vetting has been authorised.

(2) Defence can challenge '**for cause**', which, in terms of a Practice Note issued by the Lord Chief Justice in 1973, may *not* include race, religion, political beliefs or occupation. A successful challenge is therefore only likely to occur where the juror is personally known. In *R v Gough* (1993), it was held that where a juror is challenged on the grounds of possible bias, the test is whether there is 'real danger' that he or she is biased. Note that the right of the defence to use peremptory challenges was abolished by the **Criminal Justice Act 1988**.

(3) Both parties may challenge the whole jury panel — '**challenge to the array**' — on the grounds that the summoning officer is biased or has acted improperly. This happens rarely.

The process of **jury vetting** is conducted by the prosecution with the written permission of the Attorney General and involves checking the list of potential jurors to see if anyone appears 'unsuitable'. This matter first came to the attention of the public in 1978 in the *ABC* trial, a case brought under the **Official Secrets Act 1911**, when it emerged that vetting had been authorised by the Attorney General. Guidelines have since been published, which stated that vetting is only justifiable in exceptional cases, such as those involving terrorism, the Official Secrets Acts and 'professional' criminals.

The function of the jury

Jurors have to weigh up the evidence and decide what the true facts of the case are. The judge directs them as to what the relevant law is, and they must then apply that law to the facts that they have found and thereby reach a verdict.

In civil cases, if the jury has found the defendant liable, it then decides on the amount of damages to award. In any case involving a jury, there is a partnership between the judge, who acts as 'master of the law', and the jury, which is 'master of the facts'.

Criminal cases

Juries are used in all serious criminal cases, that is indictable offences tried at Crown Court. The jury has the sole responsibility for determining guilt. Since the **Criminal Justice Act 1967**, majority verdicts are possible (a minimum of ten out of 12 must agree).

During the trial, after being sworn in, jurors are present to hear all the evidence put forward in the case by the prosecution and defence counsels. Notes may be taken and jurors have the opportunity to question witnesses through the judge.

At the end of the case for the defence and after the closing speeches of counsel, the judge summarises the evidence in the case and directs the jury on relevant legal issues. In complicated cases, the judge also provides a structured set of questions to assist the jury in its deliberations. The jury retires to a private room, where it chooses a foreperson to present its verdict. If the jury has not returned with a unanimous verdict after a minimum period of 2 hours 10 minutes, the judge may recall it and advise that a majority verdict may be made under the **Criminal Justice Act 1967** (about 20% of convictions each year are given by such verdicts).

Are juries representative?

The justification for the use of juries in serious criminal cases is that the 12 people are selected randomly and should therefore comprise a representative sample of the population. This ideal has come closer with the abolition of the property qualification and the use of computers for random selection. However, it has been argued that random selection might make a jury *less* likely to be representative: if, for example, many women are excused through childcare commitments, summoning twice as many women as men might be a better way of achieving a representative section of the community.

Research carried out by Michael Zander in 1983 found that women were only slightly under-represented and that non-white people constituted 5% of juries (they made up 5.9% of the national population). While this last point is encouraging, the Commission for Racial Equality has argued that consideration should be given to the racial balance in particular cases. The Commission suggests that, where a case has a racial dimension and the defendant reasonably believes that he or she cannot receive a fair trial from an all-white jury, the judge should have the power to order that three of the jurors come from the same ethnic minority as the defendant or the victim. This recommendation was endorsed by the Runciman Royal Commission on Criminal Justice but has never been implemented; the decision in R v Ford (1989) that there is no principle that a jury should be racially balanced still holds. It is also endorsed by Lord Justice Auld in his Criminal Justice Review but has not been accepted by the government.

In recent years, the representative nature of juries has been threatened by the considerable number of professional people evading jury service. Figures show that in some courts, more than one third of people who are asked to sit on juries avoid service. The problem is particularly acute with cases that are likely to last for 5 weeks or more, especially complex fraud trials. This is the reason why, as a result of the **Criminal Justice Act 2003**, it is now more difficult for jurors to be excused from jury service.

Advantages of jury trial

Public participation

Juries allow the ordinary citizen to take part in the administration of justice, so that verdicts are seen to be those of society rather than of the judicial system. This satisfies the constitutional tradition of judgement by one's peers. Lord Denning described jury service as giving 'ordinary folk their finest lesson in citizenship'. Lord Carswell also affirmed the view that juries demonstrate democracy in action when he said: 'The institution of jury trial with all its imperfections is still trusted by the public as a method of determining the guilt of persons charged with criminal offences.'

A survey commissioned by the Bar Council and the Law Society found that:
- over 80% of those questioned were likely to have more confidence in juries than in other players in the justice system
- over 80% thought that juries were likely to reflect their views and values
- 85% trusted juries to reach the right decision
- 85% thought that juries improved the quality of the justice system

These findings have particular importance when one considers the background of magistrates, who continue to be predominantly white and middle class.

Layman's equity

Because juries have the ultimate right to find defendants innocent or guilty, it is argued that they act as a check on officialdom and protect against unjust or oppressive prosecution by reflecting a community's sense of justice. Michael Mansfield QC argues: 'It is the most democratic form of justice in the world, a protection against the use of overbearing and arbitrary power by governments.' By 'bending the law', juries, unlike judges and magistrates, have the power to acquit a defendant where the law demands a guilty verdict. There are several well-known cases of juries using this right to find according to their consciences, often in cases dealing with issues of political and moral controversy, e.g. *R v Ponting* (1985), *R v Kronlid* (1996) and *R v Owen* (1992). The importance of this aspect of the jury's involvement in criminal justice is difficult to assess. In high-profile cases such as *Ponting*, it can be a valuable statement of public feeling to those in authority, but it cannot always be relied upon. In *R v Tisdall* (1984), the defendant exposed government wrongdoing by leaking information. Although it was admitted that the leak was no threat to national security, she was convicted, unlike Ponting, who had done the same thing.

Better 'decision making'

On the key issue of deciding guilt or innocence, it can be argued that even criminal cases that involve complex issues of law come down to a consideration of essential facts, e.g. identification, witness credibility and dishonesty (in a theft case). Such matters are more likely to be decided correctly as a result of discussion between unbiased and legally unqualified people than by a single judge. Individual jurors form different impressions about the truthfulness of various witnesses and the legal arguments submitted by opposing counsel. It is also suggested that, because most jurors sit only once in criminal trials, they are not 'case-hardened' and take their responsibility seriously.

Disadvantages of juries

Lack of competence

Sir Frederick Lawton once stated that jurors' 'level of understanding of cases, and perhaps their level of intelligence, are not always up to the task they have to perform'. Lord Denning, too, argued that the selection of jurors is too wide, resulting in juries that are not competent to perform their tasks. He went on to suggest that jurors should be selected in much the same way as magistrates, through interviews and references. This throws up several obvious problems: it would be a complicated and expensive process, and a jury that is intelligent and educated can still be biased. Furthermore, the essential argument in favour of juries — that they are randomly selected — would be destroyed.

Particular concern has been expressed about the average jury's understanding of complex fraud cases. In 1986, the Roskill Committee concluded that trial by random jury was not a satisfactory way of achieving justice in such cases, since many jurors were 'out of their depth'. Terence Ingman points out that through 'inexperience and ignorance', jurors may rely too heavily on what they are told by lawyers at the expense of the real issues. However, the Roskill Committee could not find accurate evidence of a higher proportion of acquittals in complex fraud cases than in any other kind of case. In fact, researchers Smith and Bailey found that juries are capable of coming to reasoned and fair verdicts even in complex cases, and police evidence before the Runciman Royal Commission stated that in serious fraud trials, the jury actually convicts a slightly higher percentage of cases. In a recent serious fraud trial — *R v Rayment and Others,* which collapsed in 2005 after many months and a cost of over £60 million — an inquiry conducted by HM Chief Inspector of the Crown Prosecution Service, Stephen Wooler, concluded that 'a better monument to the endeavours of juries in this country or a better justification for the jury system would be hard to find'. In a research study undertaken into this case by Professor Sally Lloyd-Bostock, it was stated that the jury 'did indeed have a good grasp of the evidence'. Jurors did not appear to have had problems understanding the evidence or essentials of the case, despite the length of the trial — 21 months.

Although both Conservative and Labour governments have tried to remove jury trials for fraud cases, such has been the strength of arguments by lawyers and judges that no changes have been made.

Jury nobbling

Despite the introduction of majority verdicts in the **Criminal Justice Act 1967**, it is believed that jury nobbling remains a major weakness. Jury nobbling is an attempt made by means of threats or bribery to 'persuade' a juror to return a 'not-guilty' verdict. In 1982, several Old Bailey trials had to be stopped because of attempted nobbling. In 1984, jurors in the *Brinks Mat* trial had to have police protection to and from the court, and their telephone calls were intercepted. A new criminal offence of intimidating or threatening to harm jurors was introduced in the **Criminal Procedure and Investigation Act 1996** to try to give additional protection to juries. More radically, s.54 of that Act provided that, where a person has been acquitted and someone is later convicted of interfering with or intimidating jurors or witnesses in the case, the High Court can quash the acquittal and the person can be retried.

Bias

Ingman suggests that jurors may be biased for or against certain groups, e.g. the police. However, in a group of 12 jurors, it is likely that individual bias will be cancelled out. The most conspicuous instance of jury bias has appeared in libel cases where juries prejudiced against tabloid newspapers have awarded huge damages against them, e.g. *Sutcliffe* v *Pressdram* (1990).

Cost

One argument against juries is that jury trials in the Crown Court are more expensive than trials in the Magistrates' Court. However, by far the greatest expense in the Crown Court is the cost of lawyers, judges and other court personnel. Most criminal trials last no more than a day, and the maximum jury cost for that is only £500.

Difficulties with appeals

When judges sit alone, their judgement consists of a detailed and explicit finding of fact. When there is a jury, the verdict is returned unexplained as, under s.8 of the **Contempt of Court Act 1981**, jury deliberations are secret.

Magistrates

About 30,000 lay magistrates try more than 2 million cases a year — over 96% of all criminal cases — while about 130 District Judges (Magistrates' Courts) with a 7-year general advocacy qualification (formerly called stipendiaries) are appointed by the queen on the recommendation of the Lord Chancellor.

Selection and appointment

Under the **Justices of the Peace Act 1997**, lay magistrates are appointed by the Lord Chancellor on the advice of county local advisory committees. Members of these committees, mostly drawn from the magistracy, are appointed by the Lord Chancellor. They are supposed to have good local knowledge and to represent a balance of political opinion. Until recently, candidates for positions as magistrates were nominated by various organisations, such as local political parties, voluntary groups and trade unions. However, nowadays candidates must make a formal application — either in response to an advertisement or by making an enquiry through the government website.

The only qualifications for appointment to the magistracy are that the applicants must be aged between 18 and 65 and they are expected to live or work within the local justice area to which they are allocated. For many years Lord Chancellors would not appoint people under the age of 27 as it was felt that they did not possess the necessary experience. However, in recent years a number of younger magistrates have been appointed, including a 21-year-old disc jockey in Horsham and a 19-year-old law student in Pontefract.

Applicants must be able to devote, on average, half a day a week to the task, for which only expenses and a small loss of earnings allowance are given. Certain people are excluded from the magistracy: police officers, traffic wardens, probation officers and members of their immediate families; members of the armed forces; those with certain criminal convictions; and undischarged bankrupts.

In 1998, the Lord Chancellor revised the procedures for appointing lay magistrates, aiming to make the criteria open and clear. A job description was introduced, which states that the six key qualities defining the personal suitability of candidates are:
- good character
- understanding and communication
- social awareness
- maturity and sound temperament
- sound judgement
- commitment and reliability

The advisory committee arranges interviews for shortlisted candidates after their references have been checked. There are two interviews: the first examines the candidate's character; the second, comprising sentencing and trial exercises, assesses the candidate's judgement. After the interviews, potential appointees are reviewed by the local advisory committee to ensure that a 'balanced bench' can be achieved in terms of age, gender, ethnic background and occupation. The committee submits its recommendations to the Lord Chancellor, who usually accepts them and makes the appointment. The final stage is the 'swearing-in' of new magistrates by a senior circuit judge.

Magistrates can be removed by the Lord Chancellor at any time, but only in cases where an individual is deemed to have misbehaved or acted in a way that is inconsistent with the office. Magistrates usually have to retire at 70.

Training

Training is organised by the Judicial Studies Board and is carried out by a team of legal advisers, supported by appropriate professionals such as psychiatrists, probation officers, lawyers and judges. On appointment, all magistrates receive an intensive induction course to familiarise them with court procedures and the theory and practice of sentencing. Since 1998, the amount of training has intensified, with the appointment of experienced magistrates as mentors who support the training and development organised under the Magistrates National Training Initiative (MNTI 2) programme. New magistrates are assessed within 2 years of their appointment to ensure they have acquired the necessary competencies.

Magistrates who sit in youth courts or on family court panels receive additional training, as do magistrates who wish to become court chairpersons. As new laws dealing with sentencing are passed, more resources are needed for magistrate training, in terms of both time and financial expenditure.

Criminal jurisdiction

Lay magistrates have four main functions in criminal cases:
- **(1)** hearing applications for bail (**Bail Act 1976**) and legal aid
- **(2)** trying all summary offences and the majority of 'either-way' offences; they are advised on points of law by legally qualified clerks, but they alone decide the facts, interpret the law and, where they convict, decide the sentence and any costs and compensation
- **(3)** dealing with appeals: in ordinary appeals against conviction and/or sentence from the Magistrates' Courts to the Crown Court, magistrates (usually two) sit with a circuit judge
- **(4)** dealing with requests for arrest and search warrants from the police

Youth court
The proceedings in the youth court are similar to but less formal than those in the adult courts. They are held in the presence of three magistrates and the justice's clerk. The magistrates concerned in youth courts must have received additional training and there must be a mixed-gender bench. A parent or guardian must be present, and the youth may be accompanied by a legal representative or social worker.

Unlike the adult court, the hearing is held in private and the defendant's name is not disclosed to the public unless it is in the public interest. If found guilty, the young person is either bound over or receives a deferred sentence, a community sentence or (only if he or she is over 15) a sentence of detention in a young offenders' institution. If the offender is aged 12–14, convicted of a sufficiently serious offence and judged to be a persistent offender, a new sentence under the **Criminal Justice and Public Order**

Act 1994 may be given — a detention and training order (maximum 2 years, of which 12 months requires the defendant to be under supervision).

Other sentences include a fine, absolute or conditional discharge, an antisocial behaviour order (ASBO) or an attendance centre order (for 10–20-year-olds). A referral order is relevant only for first-time offenders who have pleaded guilty; it is set at between 3 and 12 months, depending on the seriousness of the offence. The referral is to a local youth offender panel, which draws up a 'contract' of aims targeted at addressing the offending behaviour. A defendant aged between 10 and 17 can be issued with a supervision order, whereby a social worker is to 'advise, assist and befriend'.

Procedure for indictable offences

Section 51 of the **Crime and Disorder Act 1998** states that for indictable-only offences, adults appearing in the Magistrates' Court should 'be sent forthwith' to the Crown Court. Submissions of 'no case to answer' are now part of the pre-trial procedure at the Crown Court. This process removes the former committal powers of magistrates in such cases.

Civil jurisdiction

Licensing court

Under the Licensing Act 2003, magistrates have an appellate jurisdiction in dealing with applications for licences for the sale of alcohol, and in licensing gaming establishments.

Family court

Since the implementation in 1991 of the **Children Act 1989**, the magistrates' family proceedings courts have worked in parallel with the County Courts. Cases are usually assigned to the County Courts on the grounds of legal complexity, conflicting expert opinion or high profile. Family courts deal with care orders, supervision orders and emergency protection orders. They also have jurisdiction over parental responsibility and contact orders. Adoptions come to the family court for the making of final orders.

Civil debt enforcement

Payment of debts such as council tax or utility (water, gas and electricity) bills is enforced by magistrates.

Powers of magistrates

The maximum term of imprisonment that can be imposed by magistrates is 6 months, unless there are two or more charges that can carry a term of imprisonment, in which case a total of 12 months can be imposed. The maximum fine that magistrates can impose is £5,000. In the youth court, magistrates have the power to sentence a young offender to 2 years' youth custody. It should be noted that in no other European jurisdiction do lay judges have so much power.

Justices' clerks and legal advisers

Because lay magistrates are not legally qualified and possess only an elementary knowledge of criminal law, it is the function of the justices' clerk or the legal adviser to sit in court with the magistrates' bench, to administer the court and to advise the justices on points of administrative and substantive law and on sentencing. Nationally, there are about 250 full-time justices' clerks to run the courts and approximately 1,300 legal advisers, of whom 25% are sufficiently legally qualified to act as deputies to the justices' clerks. The qualification for a justices' clerk is 5 years' standing as a barrister or solicitor.

Note that in R v Eccles Justices (1989) the Queen's Bench divisional court ruled that the magistrates' decision could not stand because the legal adviser had acted outside his powers when he retired with the magistrates for 25 of the 30 minutes of their retirement from the courtroom. The suggestion was that he participated in the decision-making process.

District judges

District judges in Magistrates' Courts are legally qualified, paid judges, who have been barristers or solicitors for at least 7 years. They are appointed to courts in large cities or within a county. Retirement is at the age of 70, unless the Lord Chancellor permits an extension.

Advantages of the magistracy

Cost

Because lay magistrates are volunteers, the system is extremely cost-effective. In 2003/04, their expenses amounted to only £15 million — an average of £500 per magistrate. In 1989, the system cost about £200 million per year to run and brought in a total income of almost £270 million in fines.

Lay magistrates try the majority of criminal cases. To pay professional judges to deal with such an enormous caseload would be hugely expensive — at least £100 million per year in salaries alone, plus the cost of appointment and training — and it would take a long time to appoint and train the required number of legally qualified candidates. Switching to Crown Court trials would be even more expensive.

Lay involvement

This point is substantially the same as that cited in support of the jury (layman's equity, see pp. 60–61), but the true value of lay involvement is open to doubt because of the restricted social background of magistrates. However, because magistrates usually live within a reasonable distance of the court, this may provide them with a better-informed picture of local life than judges might have. A further important point is the diversity of magistrates, whereas lack of diversity remains a serious problem with professional judges: almost half of magistrates are female and around 8.5% are appointed from ethnic minorities.

Weight of numbers

The simple fact that magistrates usually sit in threes may make a balanced view more likely — in a real sense they sit as a 'mini-jury'.

Disadvantages of the magistracy

Inconsistency

There is considerable inconsistency in the decision making of different benches, particularly noticeable in the awards of legal aid and the types of sentence ordered. Research has confirmed that some benches are over ten times more likely to impose a custodial sentence than neighbouring benches for similar offences.

Bias towards the police

Police officers are frequent witnesses and become well known to magistrates. It has been argued that this results in an almost automatic tendency to believe police evidence. In *R* v *Bingham JJ ex parte Jowitt* (1974), a speeding case where the only evidence was that of the motorist and a policeman, the chairman of the bench said that where there was direct conflict between the defendant and the police 'my principle...has always been to believe the evidence of the police officer'. The conviction was quashed because of this remark, which was severely criticised.

'Cheap/amateur' justice argument

Because the chances of acquittal are substantially higher in the Crown Court than in the Magistrates' Court, the suspicion is created that the Crown Court is a fairer forum or even that magistrates are not as fair as they might be. It should be noted, however, that over 90% of defendants plead guilty in Magistrates' Courts, and the nature of most cases depends more on factual issues (e.g. drink-driving) than complex legal problems.

Increasing complexity of the law

Many crimes are being downgraded to summary offences, and new offences are being created. Sentencing has become more complex in recent years, with the introduction of curfew orders and ASBOs, for example.

Legal professions

In England and Wales, there are two distinct legal professions — barristers and solicitors — and two 'subsidiary' professions — licensed conveyancers and legal executives.

Solicitors

Qualifications

Usually, solicitors have a university degree, but not necessarily a law degree. Any other degree or a non-qualifying law degree has to be followed by the Graduate Diploma in

Law (GDL) — a 1-year full-time course, or 2 years part time. After the law degree or GDL, those wanting to become solicitors take the Legal Practice Course (LPC), and then undertake a 2-year training contract with a firm of solicitors, during which they have to complete a 20-day professional skills course. With these qualifications, individuals are entered onto the rolls of the Law Society and are entitled to practise as solicitors. After qualifying, solicitors have to continue their professional development by attending various courses.

While the majority of solicitors who qualify each year are graduates, it is possible to qualify as a fellow of the Institute of Legal Executives and then pass the LPC: approximately 17% of solicitors qualify this way.

Work

Most of the work of a solicitor involves giving legal advice to clients and carrying out administrative tasks, including conveyancing (dealing with the legal requirements of buying and selling property) and probate (drafting wills and acting as executors for the estates of deceased persons). Other routine work includes drawing up various kinds of contract, setting up companies and advising clients on family law problems.

Solicitors can act as advocates and represent clients in both Magistrates' and County Courts, in which they have 'rights of audience'. The opportunity to obtain rights of audience in the higher courts (Crown and High Court, and appellate courts) was first made possible by the **Courts and Legal Services Act 1990**, and was extended in the **Access to Justice Act 1999**. For rights of audience, solicitors have to qualify as solicitor-advocates. There are currently over 2,000 solicitor-advocates (out of a total number of 86,000 solicitors).

Solicitors as a group actually do more advocacy work than barristers, since 97% of all criminal cases are tried in Magistrates' Courts, where both the prosecuting and the defending lawyer are solicitors. Even where a barrister has been instructed to represent the client in a court case, the solicitor still has an important role in the overall litigation process, handling various procedural aspects of the case such as evidence gathering and discovery of documents.

Solicitors usually work in partnerships. There has been a trend in recent years for firms of solicitors to merge into larger partnerships, which in turn has led to increasing specialisation.

Barristers

Qualifications

Barristers must be graduates, although their degree need not be in law (if it is not, they must take the GDL).

In order to continue their professional training, potential barristers must become a member of one of the four Inns of Court — Gray's Inn, Lincoln's Inn, Inner Temple or Middle Temple — which are all based in London. The Inns are independent of one another and all have libraries, award scholarships and organise lectures and 'moots' (mock trials). Before being 'called to the Bar' by his or her Inn, the student must be accepted for and complete the Bar Vocational Course (BVC), which teaches the practical skills of advocacy and drafting pleadings and negotiation; the student must also have 'dined in' on 12 occasions (this rule now includes attending residential courses).

Having been called to the Bar on passing the BVC, the student must obtain a 1-year pupillage at a set of chambers with an experienced barrister, who acts as a 'pupil master'. After the first 6 months of pupillage, barristers can appear in court in minor cases by themselves. A programme of continuing education is organised by the Bar Council during this period. To practise as an independent barrister (as a member of the Bar), the barrister finally has to secure a tenancy in a set of chambers. Both processes (obtaining a pupillage and securing a tenancy) are difficult, as demand outstrips supply. There are currently no more than 650 pupillages and 300–350 tenancies available.

Work

Barristers belong to a 'referral profession': this means that members of the public usually consult a solicitor first, who will then instruct a barrister if it is considered necessary. This process is similar to that of seeing a general practitioner first with a medical problem, and then being referred by the GP to a hospital consultant if the problem is serious. Barristers may, however, be engaged directly by certain professionals, such as accountants, and, since 1996, by members of the public whose cases have been handled by Citizens Advice Bureaux staff.

In 2004, the Bar Council permitted **Direct Public Access** (DPA), whereby for the first time any individual or company may go to a barrister directly for advice in civil law matters, provided the barrister has undertaken a qualifying course run by the College of Law. If such cases require a solicitor to undertake work that a barrister is not allowed to — for example, to collect evidence or correspond with the other side — then the barrister must direct the client to a solicitor. This change does not cover criminal, family or immigration work, so a large section of the Bar is not affected. However, barristers say it is of benefit 'in a wide range of civil and tax work'.

Barristers are obliged under the **'cab-rank' rule** to accept any case referred to them, provided it lies within their legal expertise, the appropriate fee has been agreed and they are available at the time to accept the brief. This means that barristers cannot refuse to accept instructions in a case on the grounds of their own beliefs, the nature of the case or the character of the person on whose behalf they are instructed.

Most of the work of barristers involves advocacy in any court, as they have full rights of audience in all English courts. The other main activity of barristers is that of providing counsel's opinions to solicitors on behalf of clients who require a specialised second opinion.

Barristers are self-employed and work from a set of chambers with other barristers, who share administrative and accommodation expenses. A clerk is employed, whose work involves booking cases and negotiating fees.

After 10 years in practice, barristers may apply to the Lord Chancellor to become a Queen's Counsel or QC, which is called 'taking silk' as they wear a court gown made of silk. Approximately 10% of barristers are QCs. Becoming a QC is a required step for most barristers if they aspire to be circuit or High Court judges. The selection of QCs is now the responsibility of a new body called the **Queen's Counsel Appointments Company**, set up by the Law Society and the Bar Council. There are nine members on the selection panel, which is chaired by a lay person. The panel comprises two senior barristers, two senior solicitors, one judicial member and three lay/independent members.

The new selection procedures aim to be more transparent than the previous 'secret soundings' system. Candidates are required to complete an application form, which includes a self-assessment section that allows them to provide evidence against certain published competences. If the candidate passes this stage, eight references will then be taken up by the panel — four by interview and four in writing. The referees include judges before whom the candidate has appeared and other practitioners. Three further references are also taken from professional clients.

When the selection panel has made its decisions, its list of successful candidates is sent to the Lord Chancellor, who has no power to veto any candidate's name or to insert additional names.

In July 2006, the first batch of QCs appointed under the new selection system was announced. There had been 443 applications for silk, from which 175 were appointed. Significantly, of these 33 were women, ten were from ethnic minorities and four were solicitors. In the previous appointment list in 2003, only nine female applicants and seven ethnic-minority applicants were appointed, and only one solicitor. In this application round, some 30 successful applicants had no references from High Court or more senior judges at all.

Legal executives

Most firms of solicitors employ legal executives, who do much of the basic work of solicitors — especially conveyancing and probate. Their qualifications are laid down by the Institute of Legal Executives (ILEX). Trainee legal executives have to pass Parts I and II of ILEX and then work for 5 years in a firm of solicitors or other legal organisation, for example the Crown Prosecution Service (CPS), in order to become a Fellow of ILEX.

The role of professional bodies

The Law Society

The Law Society has a number of functions. It regulates admission, qualifications and training, including continuing professional development, for all solicitors and issues practising certificates. It promotes the interests of solicitors and deals with disciplinary matters and complaints.

Discipline

Following heavy criticism from the Legal Services Ombudsman and the Lord Chancellor about the Law Society's handling of client complaints, and the publication of the Clementi Report into legal services, the Law Society decided to create a completely independent complaints handling service. This is now overseen by the **Solicitors Regulation Authority** (SRA), which was set up in 2007. This body is independent and has a governing body of 16 members — nine solicitors and seven lay members. Its budget of £50 million is raised from the practising certificate fee paid annually by all solicitors.

Complaints from the public are sent to the **Legal Complaints Service** (LCS). After investigation, if it is decided that the complaint is justified, the solicitor against whom the complaint was made can be ordered to reduce his or her bill, pay compensation up to £15,000 or correct a mistake that he or she has made and pay any costs involved. If the complaint is found to be serious, involving dishonesty or the breach of any other rule of professional conduct, it may be referred by the LCS to the SRA. In such cases, the complaint could then be referred to the **Solicitors Disciplinary Tribunal**, which has statutory powers to discipline the solicitor by fining him or her, or even striking him or her off the roll of the Law Society, effectively 'sacking' the solicitor. In recent years, more solicitors are being struck off than ever before. Appeals from this tribunal go to the High Court.

The Bar Council

The Bar Council has overall control of practising barristers, and its members come from all sections of the Bar. Its functions include making general policy decisions, determining the consolidated regulations for the Inns of Court, dealing with disciplinary matters and making provisions for the education and training of barristers.

Discipline

In 1997, the Bar Council appointed its first Complaints Commissioner, who can require barristers to reduce, refund or waive fees and can order compensation of up to £15,000. More serious complaints will be referred to the Bar Standards Board, which can decide to dismiss the complaint or to find the barrister guilty of misconduct. It has the power to fine barristers up to £5,000 or to suspend or disbar them. In 2000, in a major change of the law, the case of *Hall* v *Simons* overturned the earlier case of *Rondel* v *Worsley* (1969), thus removing barristers' immunity from being sued for professional negligence in respect of work in court.

Legal Services Ombudsman

Complainants who are dissatisfied with the way in which their grievances are handled by either profession can ask the Ombudsman to investigate. In 2005–06, the Ombudsman reported investigating 1,664 new cases, most dealing with complaints against solicitors. These made up 89.1% of referrals. Although an improvement in the percentage of satisfactory investigations was reported (from 62% to 66.4%), it was noted that 'the overall performance is well short of where a modern consumer-focused organisation should be'. During the year, adverse findings were recorded in 492 of the 1,701 reports issued, and 92 cases were sent back to the Law Society to be re-investigated. It was recommended that the Law Society paid compensation amounting to £143,645 in a total of 330 cases.

Social background of lawyers

The legal profession as a whole has traditionally come from a narrow social background in terms of class, race and sex. This is, of course, a problem in several other areas of professional life in the UK. In the law, as elsewhere, the main disadvantage of this social barrier is that it prevents the profession from attracting the best minds that the country has to offer. It also means that the legal system is sometimes seen as elitist and unapproachable, which can deter some people from using legal representation to defend their rights. The judiciary is drawn from the legal professions and this tends to produce judges with a similarly narrow background

Lawyers are mainly middle class. Evidence to the Royal Commission on Legal Services (RCLS) stated that the parental occupation of 60.9% of its solicitor students and 67.3% of its bar students was either professional or managerial.

A major contributory factor to this situation has been the lack of funding for legal training, which has made it difficult for students without wealthy parents to qualify, especially as barristers. In recent years, the difficulties have worsened, as a shortage of funds has meant that local education authorities (LEAs) have become more reluctant to award discretionary grants even to cover fees, let alone living expenses. A survey by the Law Society in 1992 found that of the 102 LEAs that replied, only six would consider giving discretionary grants to students on the GDL course and 57 to students on the LPC. Even these did not undertake to give grants to all applicants; and grants, when given, rarely covered more than a percentage of tuition fees. Maintenance grants were only given in exceptional circumstances and would cover only a percentage of living expenses.

Women remain under-represented in both legal professions, although in terms of entry women now make up 62% of Law Society entrants, 59% of trainee solicitors and about 50% of new barristers. However, there are significant problems when one considers the relatively few women who are QCs or partners in solicitors' firms. In 1996, a survey by the Law Society found that differences in pay ranged from an average of £3,000 between male and female assistant solicitors, to as much as £15,000 between men and women at partner level. At the Bar, only 33 out of the 175 new QCs in 2007 were women. Only three judges (out of 37) in the Court of Appeal and ten (out of 108) High Court judges are women.

Major changes in the legal professions

Solicitors
- Under the **Administration of Justice Act 1985**, monopoly conveyancing rights were removed and licensed conveyancers were created.
- Under the **Courts and Legal Services Act 1990**, higher-court rights of audience are granted to solicitor-advocates. There are now over 2,000 solicitor-advocates. Note Linklaters' announcement in 2001 that all litigation lawyers in the firm are to qualify as solicitor-advocates, and that virtually all litigation will be 'in-house'. Higher judicial appointments have been opened up to solicitors. Multidisciplinary partnerships have become a possibility, subject to the regulations of the Law Society.
- There is increasing specialisation within the profession; continuing professional development (CPD) is required.
- There has been a trend for smaller firms to merge and a movement towards international partnerships. Clifford Chance has become the world's largest firm of solicitors.
- The number of female applicants is increasing: 52% of new solicitors in 1998 were women.
- Nowadays, the majority of top law graduates from Oxbridge enter the solicitors' profession, not the Bar.
- The complaints process is much improved. The Legal Complaints Service has been established.
- The **Access to Justice Act 1999** should lead to full rights of audience for solicitors, once the Law Society provides specialist advocacy training.

Barristers
- There is now direct professional access: certain professions, e.g. accountants, can consult barristers directly without being referred by solicitors.
- There is Direct Public Access to barristers.
- Rules on the location of sets of chambers in London have been relaxed: previously barristers could only work in Inns of Court.
- The number of women entrants to the Bar is increasing — now almost 50%.
- There are more female judges.
- There is greater specialisation and CPD.
- There are more female QCs: 33 were appointed in 2007.
- A woman has been appointed as a Law Lord for the first time — Dame Brenda Hale.
- The post of Complaints Commissioner has been created to deal with complaints against barristers.
- *Hall* v *Simons* overturned the ruling in *Rondel* v *Worsley*: barristers and solicitors can now be sued for negligence in court work.

- Rules against employed barristers having rights of audience are being relaxed. Crown Prosecution Service barristers and solicitor-advocates are now allowed to prosecute in Crown Courts. In July 2001, the Director of Public Prosecutions (DPP) prosecuted in a Crown Court trial for the first time. In September 2001, the Bar Council advised the Lord Chancellor that it had dropped its objection to employed barristers having rights of audience.
- Barristers may now advertise — discreetly.
- In 2001, the Bar Council approved salaries for pupil barristers.

Finance of advice and representation

Society requires that all its members keep the law. It therefore follows that all citizens should not only be equally bound by the legal system but also be equally served by it. Yet almost a century ago, Lord Justice Mathew commented: 'In England, justice is open to all — like the Ritz Hotel.' In other words, anyone can go there, but only if they can afford it. One of the most serious issues that has always confronted our legal system is access to justice — how people can obtain appropriate legal advice and then take a case to court when legal costs are so high.

Since the end of the Second World War, the state has tried to provide a comprehensive system of free or subsidised legal advice and representation. The introduction of such schemes was described by a senior judge as one of the major legal reforms of the twentieth century. However, since the 1990s, the bill for this system of legal aid has increased tremendously, from a figure of about £400 million to the present level of £2 billion. Despite government efforts to 'tighten up' means tests, particularly with the Green Form legal advice scheme in 1993, costs continued to outstrip its ability to fund the system.

The financial limits of legal aid and advice schemes combined with the high fees charged by lawyers mean that large numbers of the population are unable to access legal advice. This is referred to as the 'unmet need for legal services': only the very rich, through paying privately, or the very poor, through legal aid, are capable of taking cases to court.

You need to be aware of the different ways of funding legal advice and legal representation, both in criminal and civil matters:
- paying privately for a solicitor or barrister
- private legal insurance
- motor or house insurance policies
- 'law for free' work by lawyers (formerly called 'pro bono')
- Citizens Advice Bureaux (CAB)
- law centres

- independent advice centres — Age Concern, Shelter
- local authority services — Trading Standards, Environmental Health, housing advice centres, welfare rights units
- Race Equality Councils
- trade union or professional associations
- the Free Representation Unit in London, which handles 1,000 tribunal cases a year on a *pro bono* basis
- ALAS — the Law Society's free Accident Legal Advice Service, aimed at helping accident victims recover compensation
- state-funded legal aid

The **Access to Justice Act 1999** created the Legal Services Commission (LSC), an executive agency with overall responsibility for state funding of advice and representation. This replaced the Legal Aid Board. In contrast to the previous system, the commission has been given a fixed annual budget (currently around £2 billion per year) and allocates funding to the Criminal Defence Service (responsible for criminal matters) and the Community Legal Service (responsible for civil matters). The Criminal Defence Service (CDS) takes priority in the allocation of funding; it is a demand-led scheme and all eligible persons will be funded. If necessary, funds will be transferred from the Community Legal Service (CLS) budget to pay for criminal work. The LSC has been given significantly more power than its predecessor and will gain much more control over publicly funded cases through the use of contracts with providers.

The civil scheme

The following schemes are run by the CLS:
- **Legal help** provides initial advice and assistance with any legal problem, but is subject to a tight means test. Help is available from a solicitor or other legal adviser who holds a contract with the Legal Services Commission. Under this scheme, legal advice up to a limit of £500 may be provided to the client.
- **Help at court** allows for a solicitor or legal adviser to speak on the client's behalf at certain court proceedings without formally acting for him or her in the whole proceedings, e.g. an application to suspend a warrant for possession in a housing case.
- **Approved family help** provides assistance in a family dispute, including facilitating a resolution through mediation.

Civil legal aid

The funding for civil legal aid is controlled by the CLS and covers all the work involved in bringing an action to court or defending an action in court, including representation. Since the **Access to Justice Act 1999**, all actions for recovery of money damages, especially personal injury cases, have been 'diverted' to conditional fee agreements — see below. Such legal aid funding as is still provided is targeted on child protection cases, cases involving breaches of human rights and social welfare cases, including housing and employment rights.

Eligibility for funding depends on a means test, which considers an applicant's disposable income and capital. Those whose income and capital are below the minimum limits will pay no contributions, but if income or capital is between the lower and upper limits, a contribution must be paid. There is also a merits test to ensure that such funding is only given where the case has a good prospect of success and where the award of damages will exceed the costs of the case.

Conditional fee agreements (CFAs)

Conditional fee agreements were first introduced into English law in 1995 under the **Courts and Legal Services Act 1990** (the implementation of the Act was delayed), which allowed a form of contingency fee. Under the CFA scheme, solicitors and barristers can agree to take no fee if they lose a case and are able, if they win, to raise their fee up to a maximum of double the usual rate. (However, under a voluntary Law Society agreement, this 'uplift' is limited to a maximum of 25% of damages recovered.) The **Access to Justice Act 1999** gave the scheme greater prominence, and the clear intention is that all claims for money damages should be made on the basis of CFAs.

In order to ensure money is available to pay the other side's legal costs if the case is lost, the Law Society has arranged an 'after-the-event' insurance scheme whereby, for a relatively small amount, the claimant's liability for such costs is covered.

Advantages of CFAs

- **No cost to the state.** The costs are entirely borne by the solicitor or the client, depending on the outcome of the case. Supporters of this scheme argue that, as well as saving public money, CFAs allow the government to fund properly those cases that still need state support and to direct more funds towards suppliers of free legal advice, such as the CAB.
- **Anyone can bring a case for damages.** One of the strongest arguments in favour of CFAs is that they allow cases to be brought by many people who would not have been eligible for legal aid or who could not reasonably have been expected to pay contributions under the existing civil legal aid scheme. As long as he or she can afford to insure against losing and can persuade a solicitor that the case is worth the risk, anyone can bring a case for damages.
- **They raise performance levels of solicitors.** Supporters of CFAs claim that conditional fees encourage solicitors to perform well since they have a financial interest in winning cases funded in this way.
- **Wider coverage.** It looks likely that CFAs may be allowed for defamation actions and cases brought before tribunals — two major gaps in the existing legal aid scheme.
- **Fairness to opponents.** Clients receiving legal aid who lost their cases were not usually obliged to pay the winning side's costs, which was seen as an unfair advantage, particularly where both litigants were ordinary individuals but only one qualified for legal aid. The insurance requirement of CFAs solves this problem.
- **Discouragement of frivolous or weak cases.** In recent years, apparently trivial cases have been dragged through the courts at public expense, seemingly confirm-

ing the view that both solicitors and the Legal Services Commission are unable to apply the merits test sufficiently rigorously. For example, a convicted bank robber received £1,500 by means of a preliminary legal aid certificate in order to bring an action against the police for a new suit to replace the one he was wearing when he was shot by police officers. Solicitors are unlikely to take on such cases, but, if they do, they or their clients bear the costs.

Disadvantages of CFAs

- **They are an inadequate substitute for legal aid in uncertain cases.** Most of those who have criticised CFAs accept that in uncertain cases they are a good *addition* to the state-funded legal aid system, but are concerned that they may not be adequate as a *substitute* for it.
- **Solicitors may only take on cases they are likely to win.** Critics, including the Bar, the Law Society and the Legal Action Group, have expressed strong concerns that certain types of case will lose out under the CFA scheme. They suggest that solicitors will only want to take on cases under CFAs where there is a high chance of winning.
- **The insurance premiums to cover losing are high.** Most concern is expressed about medical negligence cases, which are generally difficult for claimants to win — the success rate is around 17%, compared to 85% for other personal injury actions. It can often cost between £2,000 and £5,000 simply to carry out the initial investigation necessary to assess whether the case is worth pursuing. For those difficult cases, 'after-the-event' insurance can be very expensive — in one such case in 1997, the insurance premium was £15,000.
- **CFAs are inadequate for difficult cases with low awards of damages.** CFAs are unsuitable for cases of great public importance that require extensive work, are difficult to win and/or may attract relatively low levels of damages even if successful, such as litigation by cancer sufferers against tobacco companies, or actions against the police or government.
- **CFAs are valueless to some litigants.** There are obvious limitations to CFAs in that they would be of no value to some litigants. A defendant without a counterclaim cannot pay his lawyer's success fee, nor can claimants seeking a remedy other than money damages, such as an injunction for nuisance or a boundary dispute between neighbours.
- **There may be pressure to settle out of court.** The claimant may feel pressured by his or her lawyer to settle out of court (as this would guarantee the latter's uplift fee). If this happened, the claimant would potentially receive lower damages than if the case had been pursued in court. Further, while the cost of both the uplift fee and insurance premium used to be paid by the claimant, such payments can now be claimed from the defendant (since the **Access to Justice Act 1999**). This change encourages the defendant to settle out of court too.
- **CFAs are open to abuse.** Since payment depends on success, unethical practices such as 'ambulance chasing', coaching witnesses and withholding evidence might become common features of the legal landscape in the UK, as they have in American courtrooms.

- **There may be a conflict of interest between the solicitor and the client.** There is evidence in some cases that lawyers' advice about settlement may be influenced by their need to be paid rather than by the strict merits of any settlement offer. The problem could be exacerbated by the involvement of insurance companies, which, through the solicitor, could pressurise the client to accept an inadequate settlement by threatening to withdraw insurance cover against losing. There is also a possibility of solicitors cutting corners to enhance profit, which might lead to allegations of professional negligence.
- **There is public uncertainty as to what CFAs are and how the scheme operates.** In a research study entitled *Nothing To Lose* (reported in an article by Fiona Bawden, *New Law Journal*, 17 December 1999), the main finding was that clients think that CFAs are confusing. The researchers concluded:

> Only one client understood the operation of the CFA scheme in its entirety. If anyone comes across this client, they should buy him a drink!...The fact is that CFAs are a fantastically complicated way of funding litigation. They are a halfway house hybrid grafted onto the existing litigation system by a government determined to increase access to justice but too squeamish to go the whole hog and introduce US-style contingency fees. The blame for clients' lack of understanding almost certainly lies with the system itself, rather than with high-handed solicitors failing to try to explain what signing up to a CFA involves.

Criminal legal aid

Unlike legal aid in civil cases, state-funded criminal defence continues to be given on a demand-led basis. This means that, although the total legal aid budget is fixed, there is no set limit for criminal legal aid, and all cases that meet the merits and means tests are funded.

The Lord Chancellor's Department has identified the following problems that have arisen with the provision of state-funded criminal legal aid:

- The cost rose from £507 million in 1992/93 to £733 million in 1997/98 — an increase of 44%. At the same time, the number of cases dealt with increased by only 10%. The cost reached £1.158 billion in 2005/06.
- Although standard fees are now paid in many cases, the most expensive cases are paid in the traditional way, by calculating the bill after the event. This gives lawyers an incentive to boost their fees by dragging cases out, and these cases take up a disproportionate amount of money.
- The system for means-testing defendants to see whether they should contribute to the costs of their case is a waste of time and money. The test has not stopped some apparently wealthy defendants from receiving free legal aid, and 94% of defendants in the Crown Court pay no contribution at all.

Under the **Access to Justice Act 1999**, the provision of funding is the responsibility of the Criminal Defence Service (CDS), which controls two schemes:

- The **duty solicitor scheme** was originally created under the **Police and Criminal Evidence Act (PACE) 1984** to provide a right to legal advice for suspects detained in police stations. It ensures access to a solicitor for advice, and assistance is available 24 hours a day, free of charge and without means or merits tests. At Magistrates' Courts, there is normally a duty solicitor available to give free advice on a defendant's first appearance if he or she does not have his or her own solicitor.
- The **criminal legal advice scheme** works in the same way as legal help (referred to on p. 75), with the same strict means test.

Criminal legal aid covers all types of criminal proceedings and pays for a solicitor to prepare the case and represent a client in court. It also covers the cost of a barrister, particularly if the case is heard in the Crown Court. The decision to grant aid depends on the two tests outlined below.

Merits test

The court decides whether it is in the interests of justice to grant legal aid. For serious cases, such as murder or rape, it will always be in the interests of justice to provide it. For less serious cases, such as minor motoring offences, the court is unlikely to agree to it. Between these extremes, the court decides on the basis of guidelines set out in the **Legal Aid Act 1988**.

'Interests of justice' criteria include cases where:
- the charge is so serious that, if convicted, the defendant risks the loss of liberty
- complex legal issues are involved
- the defendant is unable to understand the proceedings because of language problems etc.

Means test

The court looks into the applicant's financial position and the likely cost of the case:
- Applicants with the lowest means receive free legal aid, whatever the costs of the case.
- Applicants with more substantial means will not be granted legal aid if they can afford the likely costs.
- If the likely costs are large, applicants with reasonable means may be granted legal aid, but the court can require an applicant to pay a contribution towards the cost of the case from both income and capital if he or she appears able to do so. Judges in the Crown Court are able to order convicted defendants to pay some or all of the cost of their representation. This replaces the current system of universal means testing at the start of the case in the Magistrates' Courts. If the applicant is cleared of the offence, the court normally refunds all contributions he or she may have made towards legal aid.

The Ministry of Justice has increased the powers of the Criminal Defence Service to control the quality of services provided at public expense, through contracting with private lawyers. A new body, the Public Defender Service (PDS), has also been established to provide salaried state lawyers to represent defendants in court. Defendants retain the option of having lawyers in private practice to represent them.

Criticisms of legal aid

Legal help

Formerly known as the Form 10/Green Form scheme, the legal help scheme was designed to bring in a new range of work, in part to address the issue of the unmet need for legal services for dealing with welfare and similar problems, which individuals have traditionally been reluctant to bring to lawyers. The scheme was largely failing until recently because of the increasing problems of running a profitable solicitors' firm. However, the number of welfare problems dealt with through legal help has started to increase, possibly because of the growing involvement of law centres specialising in this kind of work.

It is suggested that the initial financial limit for this scheme is too low, and an extension will always be necessary for obtaining a barrister's advice or expert reports, causing delays. There is also limited public awareness of the scheme and the areas it covers.

Legal representation

The major problem is that for most money claims, civil legal aid is not available. There is greater emphasis on the use of conditional fee agreements. Where civil legal aid is available, it is still subject to severe means testing, and most people who are eligible are required to make a significant personal contribution. Many claimants have to reject the offer of this state aid because they cannot afford the high monthly contributions demanded.

The statutory charge

The assisted person in any proceedings funded by the Legal Services Commission applies this charge to money or property 'recovered or preserved'. The charge may result in the 'claw-back' of all the claimant's damages, which, as far as the client is concerned, may make the whole action a waste of time. While the charge may be technically just — since privately funded clients also face the risk of losing all their damages to costs — to the legally aided client it does not look like a case of justice being seen to be done.

Recovery of costs

When a legally aided client loses a case, it is difficult, or often impossible, for the opponent to get costs back, as would normally happen in a civil case. This places the legally aided client at an unfair advantage. Despite some provision for payment from the Legal Services Commission, which increased after Lord Denning's recommendation in *Hanning* v *Maitland* (1970), being sued by a legally aided opponent is a severe risk for the average litigant. Consequently, justice suffers, since costs can be used as a weapon to force an early settlement.

Libel and slander

Assistance for legal representation is not available for libel and slander actions, so only the wealthy and powerful can afford to defend their reputations.

Tribunals

Assistance for tribunal actions is only available in a very few cases.

Criminal legal aid

Research by McConville (1993) suggested that the standards of legally aided criminal defence work are low. Much of it is carried out by unqualified staff, there is little investigative work and solicitors push clients towards pleading guilty rather than taking time to prepare an effective defence. Since the merits test concentrates on the seriousness of the charge and possible penalty, it is more difficult for defendants to get legal aid for minor offences; sometimes it may be difficult to know whether the merits criteria apply until after a trial has started.

The judiciary

The judiciary still consists almost exclusively of middle-aged to elderly men who worked as barristers for 20 years or more prior to their appointment. No one used to be able to become a High Court judge unless he or she was a barrister of at least 10 years' standing. This rule was changed by the **Courts and Legal Services Act 1990**, whereby appointments to the High Court could be made from those who had a 10-year High Court qualification (including solicitor-advocates) or from circuit judges in post for at least 2 years. The first High Court appointment of a solicitor — Michael Sachs, who had been a circuit judge — was made in 1994.

All Lord Justices of Appeal and Law Lords, the most senior judges, were formerly barristers. Barristers previously had the exclusive right to senior judicial posts, and the predominance of barristers among those appointed to the circuit bench has certain advantages, which are to the public interest in that barristers are expert in both the law and court procedures.

However, there have been significant changes to the qualifications and procedures for judicial appointment over recent years. The **Courts and Legal Services Act 1990** laid down the current statutory criteria for the appointment of each level of judge, but these were amended by the **Tribunals, Courts and Enforcement Act 2007**. This Act also abandoned the old rule that judicial appointments should be based on rights of audience, thus accepting the criticism that there is no reason to assume that advocacy experience translates into judicial wisdom.

The statutory criteria are now:

- **district judge** — 5 years' qualification as a solicitor or barrister, 'gaining experience by being engaged in law-related activities'
- **Recorder (part-time judge)** — 7 years' qualification as a solicitor or barrister, 'gaining experience...'
- **circuit judge** — 7 years' qualification as a solicitor or barrister or sitting as a Recorder, or 3 years as a district judge
- **High Court judge** — 7 years' qualification as a solicitor or barrister, or 2 years as a circuit judge
- **Lord Justice of Appeal** — 7 years' qualification as a solicitor or barrister, but in practice, always appointed from High Court judges
- **Lord of Appeal in Ordinary** — 15 years' qualification as a solicitor or barrister and at least 2 years holding high judicial office

Under s.50 of the **Tribunals, Courts and Enforcement Act 2007**, the Lord Chancellor may by order provide for another qualification to be relevant for judicial appointment if it is awarded by the Institute of Legal Executives or another authorised professional body. This provision could result in fellows of ILEX or patent agents or trademark attorneys being eligible for judicial appointment.

Appointment procedures

The **Judicial Appointments Commission** (JAC) — created by the **Constitutional Reform Act 2005** — was set up in April 2006 under the chairmanship of Baroness Prashar and is responsible for the selection of all judicial office holders (all judges and tribunal members). It is possible that in the future magistrates will also be selected by this commission. There are 15 commissioners, drawn from the judiciary, both legal professions, tribunals, the magistracy and the lay public. Twelve commissioners, including the chairperson, are appointed through open competition, and three are selected by the Judges' Council.

It is the responsibility of the JAC to select candidates for judicial office on merit. It does this independently of government, through fair and open competition and by encouraging a wide range of applicants.

To become a deputy district judge or a district judge, suitably qualified candidates respond to advertisements placed in newspapers, professional journals or on the Lord Chancellor's Department (LCD) website and complete an application form. References are taken up and shortlisted candidates are invited to a 1-day selection procedure, during which they are interviewed and take various tests to measure legal and procedural knowledge. They also participate in mock trials. Successful candidates are nominated by the JAC to the Lord Chancellor for appointment.

For Recorders and circuit judges, the procedure is broadly the same, with advertisements placed by the JAC in the same media as mentioned above. Suitably qualified candidates apply by filling in an application form and providing a number of personal referees. After these references are taken up, candidates are shortlisted and interviewed by a panel of members from the JAC. Successful candidates are nominated to the Lord Chancellor, who formally makes the appointment.

For appointment as a High Court judge, candidates are again required to apply to the JAC and provide references. Referees are interviewed by a panel chosen from the JAC, further references are taken up from the list of referees drawn up by the JAC and short-listed candidates are interviewed by a panel chosen from the members of the JAC. The JAC then nominates one candidate to the Lord Chancellor for appointment. In the first 'batch' of High Court appointments, 144 candidates applied, 123 men and 21 women: 94 were barristers, 43 were circuit judges and seven were solicitors. Only three applicants were from ethnic minorities. The commission shortlisted 57 — 44 men and 13 women. All 57 were interviewed by a panel, which was chaired by Baroness Prashar, the chairperson of the JAC, and included Lord Justice Auld and Sara Nathan, a lay commissioner. The panel chose 21 'to wait in the wings' — this means they are in a waiting pool, from which future High Court vacancies will be filled as they arise. The Lord Chancellor can accept the nomination, reject the nomination or ask the panel to reconsider the selection. In the case of High Court judicial appointments, the JAC has the power to decide that none of the applicants is suitable for appointment, but the Lord Chancellor can ask the commission to reconsider that decision. Since April 2006, the JAC has made 161 recommendations to the Lord Chancellor and none has been rejected.

Appointments of Lord Justices of Appeal are similar to the procedure followed for High Court appointments, with the only significant difference being in the constitution of the panel that considers the applications. Under the **Constitutional Reform Act 2005 (CRA)**, this panel must contain:
- the Lord Chief Justice (LCJ) (or a nominee of the LCJ, who must be either a Head of Division or a Lord Justice of Appeal)
- a Head of Division or Lord Justice nominated by the LCJ
- the chairperson of the JAC
- a lay member of the commission

In practice, all appointments of Lord Justices of Appeal are made from the ranks of High Court judges.

Appointments to the House of Lords Appellate Committee — to be renamed the Supreme Court under the CRA 2005 — are made under a different procedure because unlike all the other courts in which judges sit — County Court, Crown Court, High Court, Court of Appeal — the Supreme Court is a court of the UK, not merely of England and Wales. By convention, two members are from Scotland and one from Northern Ireland, and, although the CRA does not explicitly enact this convention, under s.27(8) 'the commission must ensure that between them the judges will have knowledge of, and experience in, the law of each part of the United Kingdom'.

No specific process is laid down in the statute, and therefore it is for the Commission to decide the nature of any competition for such an appointment. The Act does, however, require that part of the appointment procedure involve consulting:

- the Lord Chancellor
- the First Minister of Scotland
- the First Secretary of the Assembly of Wales
- the Secretary of State for Northern Ireland

The selection panel must comprise the president of the Supreme Court, the deputy president and one member each of the JAC for England and Wales, Scotland and Northern Ireland.

Having received a nomination of one candidate, the Lord Chancellor has the same options open to him or her as for appointments to the post of High Court judge or Lord Justice of Appeal. However, Supreme Court appointments are recommended to the queen by the prime minister, and under s.26(3), the prime minister has to accept the name provided by the Lord Chancellor. Before the CRA was passed, the prime minister could — and occasionally did — reject the candidate recommended by the Lord Chancellor, as Lord Hailsham, Conservative Lord Chancellor from 1979 to 1987, made clear in his autobiography.

Training

As all judges were formerly either barristers or solicitors, they are already highly skilled in legal knowledge and court procedure. This professional background has in the past led judges to believe that further training is unnecessary. In the UK, judges still receive less training than in other countries, where there are 'career judges' — law graduates who decide to train as judges without first qualifying as lawyers. This problem is compounded by the fact that many judges are appointed to try cases where they have no relevant expertise. It is quite common for Recorders, whose principal duty is to try 'either-way' offences in Crown Courts, to be selected from barristers or solicitors who have little criminal court experience. High Court judges are sometimes assigned to a division in which they have little direct experience.

Trainee Recorders undertake a 4-day residential course before sitting in a Crown Court. The course includes lectures, sentencing and summing-up exercises, mock trials and equal treatment training. The training is supplemented by visits to penal institutions, observations of serving judges and meetings with probation officers. Before presiding over a Crown Court trial, Recorders in training sit alongside an experienced circuit judge.

In recent years, the Judicial Studies Board has received large increases in its operating budget and has arranged more training for judges and magistrates, including courses in ethnic awareness, human rights and computer use. The Civil Procedure Rules — reforms to the civil justice system — have prompted further judicial training.

Functions

In civil courts, judges preside over the court, decide legal issues concerning admissibility of evidence and give a reasoned decision in favour of one of the parties. If the defendant is held liable, the judge decides the award of damages. In criminal cases tried in Crown Courts, he or she ensures that order is maintained, summarises evidence for the jury and directs it on relevant legal rules. If the defendant is convicted, the judge decides the sentence to be imposed. In appeal cases, judges have an important law-making role through the operation of the doctrine of precedent and statutory interpretation.

- **District judges** work in County Courts, where they preside over small claims cases and have administrative responsibilities, and in Magistrates' Courts, where they sit by themselves.
- **Recorders** (part time) and **circuit judges** work in both Crown Courts and County Courts.
- **High Court judges** are assigned on appointment to a specific division of the High Court. Queen's Bench judges go on circuit to Crown Courts, where they try all Class 1 offences (such as murder) and most Class 2 offences (all other serious offences for which a life sentence could be imposed). They may also sit in the Court of Appeal (Criminal Division), together with a Lord Justice of Appeal, usually on appeals against sentencing rather than appeals against conviction.
- **Lords Justices of Appeal** sit in the Court of Appeal, either in the Civil or Criminal Division, usually in a panel of three.
- **Law Lords** sit in the House of Lords (Appellate Committee), where they hear final appeals that must involve a point of law of 'general public importance'. Only about 70 cases are heard each year, the majority being tax cases. These judges also sit in the Judicial Committee of the Privy Council to hear cases from the few Commonwealth countries that allow such appeals to the UK, and from Scotland under the **Scotland (Devolution) Act 1998**. When the new Supreme Court is established under the **Constitutional Reform Act 2005**, the Law Lords will be appointed as Supreme Court judges and will no longer be able to sit or vote in the House of Lords.
- **Senior judges** are asked by government ministers to preside over judicial or public inquiries, e.g. the Dunblane Inquiry (Lord Cullen), the Hillsborough Football Disaster Inquiry (Mr Justice Taylor) and the Arms-to-Iraq Inquiry (Lord Scott).

Judicial independence

In the UK's legal system, great importance is attached to the idea that judges should be independent from any pressure from the government particularly, or from any political or other pressure groups. This is to guarantee that they are free to decide cases impartially (see Article 6 of the European Convention on Human Rights, incorporated into UK law by the **Human Rights Act 1998**).

Judicial independence is essential to the theory of the 'rule of law'. A. V. Dicey analysed this important concept in the nineteenth century and stated that 'no person is punishable except for a distinct breach of the law established in the courts', and not only is no one 'above the law, but...every man, whatever be his rank, is subject to the ordinary law of the realm'.

In an article in *The Times* (12 September 2005), Murray Gleeson (Chief Justice of Australia) wrote:

> An independent judiciary is vital to the political health of a society. Like good health, it is taken for granted when it exists and valued most when it is missing. Yet, as an indispensable condition of the rule of law, it affects people's lives in a way that few recognise.
>
> Judicial power is a function of government. Like all forms of governmental power, it exists for the benefit of citizens: to uphold their rights; to enforce their legitimate claims; to protect them from abuses of public authority or private strength. Judicial decisions should be impartial, based on the neutral application of legal standards, and made by people who have nothing to gain and nothing to fear.
>
> Constitutional arrangements, laws and conventions designed to support the independence of the judicial branch of government do not exist for the personal benefit of judges. They are there to sustain the integrity and credibility of the justice system.

Separation of powers

This theory of judicial independence owes its origin to French philosopher Baron de Montesquieu with his theory of the 'separation of powers'. In this, he argued that the only way to safeguard individual liberties is to ensure that the power of the state is divided between three separate and independent arms: the legislature, the executive and the judiciary. Each arm should operate independently and be checked and balanced by the other two.

The separation of powers works in the following ways:

- **Tenure of office.** In England, all judges of the Supreme Court hold office 'during good behaviour', subject to removal only by the monarch by means of an address presented by both Houses of Parliament (**Act of Settlement 1701**). This has never happened to an English judge. Under the CRA 2005, the Office for Judicial Complaints (OJC) was appointed to investigate complaints made against judges. The Lord Chancellor has laid down new procedures to investigate serious allegations made about circuit judges and other inferior judges. He retains the power of dismissal but may only exercise it following an investigation into any such allegations by a senior judge appointed by the Lord Chief Justice and further discussion with, and agreement of, the LCJ and other senior judges.
- **Judicial immunity from suit.** No judge may be sued in respect of anything done while acting in his or her judicial capacity.
- **Immunity from parliamentary criticism.** No criticism of an individual judge may be made in either House except by way of a substantive motion. Political neutrality is also preserved in that judicial salaries are charged upon the consolidated fund, which removes the opportunity for an annual debate.

Note that full-time judges are excluded from membership of the House of Commons. However, in the House of Lords, all Law Lords and the LCJ are able to speak during debates on particular bills and to vote. In recent years, a number of serving Law Lords became involved in politically contentious debates concerning the administration of justice, penal policy and civil liberties, e.g. the present LCJ, Lord Woolf, opposed the provision in the **Criminal Justice Bill 1997** for mandatory sentences. Such examples raise the obvious difficulty that the judges who were actively involved in the passage of legislation in the House of Lords might in the future be the judges who have to decide these same issues in their judicial capacity. This situation will cease when the new Supreme Court is established.

The value of judicial independence is highlighted by the increase in judicial review cases, in which judges are required to examine the legality or procedural correctness of government decisions. There have been many instances where judges have overruled the decisions of government ministers.

The independence of the judiciary is particularly necessary when judges have to chair inquiries into major cases and national events, e.g. the Profumo scandals, the Dunblane shootings, the Hillsborough disaster, the Stephen Lawrence murder and the Arms-to-Iraq controversy.

Dismissal

All judges of the Supreme Court — of High Court rank and above — hold office 'during good behaviour' and may only be dismissed by the monarch following the passing of a substantive critical motion through both Houses of Parliament. The only occasion on which this procedure has been invoked was in 1830, when an Irish judge, Sir Jonah Barrington, was dismissed for embezzlement; it has never happened to an English judge.

It is possible for a judge to be removed on grounds of incapacity — through physical or mental ill-health — but this depends on the discretion of the Lord Chancellor. When Lord Chief Justice Lord Widgery became seriously ill towards the end of his judicial career, although suffering from a serious degenerative nervous disease he remained in his job.

The only recent example of a High Court judge effectively resigning is that of Mr Justice Harman, who left his position following serious criticism for taking more than 18 months to deliver a reserved judgement in the Court of Appeal.

The **Office for Judicial Complaints** (OJC) was set up in April 2006 under the CRA 2005: 'The Lord Chancellor and the Lord Chief Justice have joint responsibility for a new system for considering and determining complaints about the personal conduct of all judicial office holders.' The OJC handles these complaints and provides assistance and advice to the Lord Chancellor and LCJ in the performance of their new joint role.

Complaints may be made to the OJC about the personal conduct of any judge, tribunal member or coroner. Examples of personal misconduct would be the use of insulting, racist or sexist language. The OJC cannot deal with any complaints about a judge's decision or about how he or she has handled a case — these matters are properly within the jurisdiction of the appeal process.

On completing its investigation of a complaint made against a judge, the OJC advises the Lord Chancellor and LCJ of its findings. They may then decide what action to take against the judge. They have the power to advise the judge as to his or her future conduct, to warn the judge, to reprimand, or even to dismiss an inferior judge. No disciplinary action may be taken against a judge unless both the Lord Chancellor and the LCJ agree the case merits it.

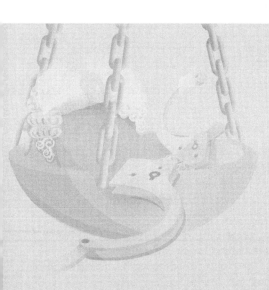

Questions
&
Answers

The new Unit 1 examination paper contains two sections: Section A — law making and Section B — the legal system.

Each section contains four three-part questions. Candidates are required to answer three questions — at least one each from Sections A and B:

- Part (a) of each question usually involves a straightforward description of the main facts of the topic (e.g. 'Describe how solicitors qualify and are trained').
- Part (b) is often an explanatory question on another issue within the topic (e.g. 'Explain how a claimant in a civil action may fund his or her claim').
- Part (c) requires analysis and evaluation (e.g. explain advantages and/or disadvantages).

Students should become familiar with the descriptors used by examiners in the award of marks for each paper:

- **Sound** — answer is generally accurate and contains material relevant to the potential content; support by references to relevant case examples and/or statutory authorities.
- **Clear** — answer is broadly accurate and relevant to the potential content, and is supported by some use of relevant case examples and/or statutory authorities.
- **Some** — answer shows some accuracy and some relevance to the potential content; few of the concepts of the potential content are established, as there are errors, omissions and/or confusion that undermine the essential features; occasional support by relevant case examples or statutory authorities.
- **Limited** — answer contains a few relevant facts with no additional explanation; no reference to case examples or statutory authorities.
- **Fragment** — answer contains one or two basic but relevant facts only; no reference to case examples or statutory authorities.

Answers marked as mainly 'sound' will achieve a grade A, whereas answers that are mainly 'clear' will achieve a B or C. Answers that are 'some' will receive a D or E.

Effective answer planning

The key difference between the A-grade and C-grade answers in this section is that the A-grade answers have a clear structure, demonstrated by a simple, accurate and relevant opening sentence and by the sequencing of the material. You are encouraged to spend time at the beginning of the examination planning your answers:

- First, read the question carefully. Are you required to outline, explain, discuss, analyse, compare or evaluate?
- Brainstorm the material you consider relevant to answer the different issues. Note down your ideas in the form of a spider diagram or under headings. This should help you to prioritise the points and indicate the links between them.
- Assess how much needs to be written on each component.
- Ensure your answer refers to case law and/or statutory authorities. Without such references, the answer will be graded as no more than 'some' or 'limited'.

Question 1

Parliamentary law making

(a) Briefly describe two influences on Parliament. (10 marks)
(b) Describe the formal process used in creating a statute. (10 marks)
(c) Discuss the advantages and disadvantages of this process. (10 marks)

■ ■ ■

A-grade answer

(a) The Law Commission was set up in 1965 to advise the government. It is a permanent, full-time body, headed by five Law Commissioners. The chairman is a High Court judge; the other four are members of the legal professions and academic lawyers. The Commission's work involves keeping all areas of law under review and producing a systematic programme of reform. The Lord Chancellor and other government departments may refer topics to it, or it may consider a topic of its choice after gaining government approval.

The Commission researches an area of law and then produces a consultative paper setting out the present law, the problems with it and any proposals for change. Interested parties are able to put forward their views and a final report is published. This sets out any recommendations and a draft bill if legislation is proposed. The bill will only become law if Parliament decides to implement it. Legislation that has resulted from this process includes the Law Reform (Year and a Day Rule) Act 1996 and the Contract (Rights of Third Parties) Act 1999. There have been over 100 proposals put forward and about 70% have been adopted.

A second area of influence is pressure groups, which are independent of Parliament. They are bodies of people with a shared interest in getting the government to change the law in certain areas. The groups may be ones with a cause, such as Shelter, Help the Aged, Friends of the Earth and Greenpeace, or groups with a sectional interest, such as the Confederation of British Industry and trade unions, and cover many different areas of concern. They try to achieve their aims by targeting politicians, civil servants and local government offices. They lobby MPs, organise petitions and gain as much publicity for their cause as possible.

Some pressure groups only exist for a short time as they are set up to deal with a specific issue. Once that issue is resolved, they disband. An example is the Snowdrop Campaign, set up after the killing of the young schoolchildren in the Dunblane massacre in 1996. A successful campaign to ban the private ownership of handguns was launched.

Some pressure groups are more successful than others. Recent examples of successful campaigns are those of ASH to bring about a ban on smoking in public places and Stonewall to legalise gay marriage (achieved in the Civil Partnership Act 2004).

 This is a thorough and detailed response with good use of examples. It displays a clear understanding of both influences. It would receive full marks.

(b) The formal process of creating a statute always involves both the House of Commons and the House of Lords. All statutes start life as a bill, and although important bills are nearly always introduced first in the Commons, bills can start their life in either House. There are two main types of bill. Public bills, the most common, are usually introduced by the government, but some are private members' bills, which are introduced by backbench MPs. The best-known example is the Abortion Act 1967. Public bills have general effect and are concerned with public policy that affects the law of the country. Private bills are usually concerned with local matters and promoted by such bodies as local authorities or statutory bodies seeking special powers.

All public bills have to undergo a formal procedure in both Houses that can start in either House. At the first reading, which is purely formal, the title of the bill is read out. At the second reading stage, the bill is proposed by the government minister responsible and the House holds a full debate on the general principles of the bill. A vote to see if the bill should go further is taken at the end of the debate. The bill then passes to the committee stage, where the committee, consisting of MPs from all the political parties, examines every clause in detail. Amendments can be made at this time. Once this is completed, the committee then reports back to the whole House, the report stage. Further amendments may be proposed and voted on. A third reading then takes place when the bill in its final form is presented to the House and the final vote is taken.

If the vote is in favour of the bill, it then passes to the other House (the House of Lords if it started in the House of Commons) and the same stages are repeated there. The difference is that in the House of Lords the whole House acts as a committee and all the amendments are debated and voted on. If the House of Lords makes amendments to a bill that started in the Commons, it is referred back to the Commons to consider the amendments. If disagreements between the Commons and Lords remain, these are usually resolved through negotiation or compromise, but ultimately the Commons has the power under the Parliament Acts 1911 and 1949 to ignore the objections of the Lords. This power is rarely used, but it was used to pass the Hunting Act 2004.

Once a bill has successfully passed through all the stages in both Houses it receives royal assent, after which it can become law. This royal assent is no longer given in person and the last time it was refused was in 1707. Without royal assent, the bill could not become law. At this point the bill becomes an Act of Parliament.

 The candidate shows sound knowledge of the roles of both Houses of Parliament and the Crown in the creation of an Act of Parliament. The difference in the procedure at the committee stage in the House of Lords is mentioned and so are the powers under the Parliament Acts. The answer would receive 10 marks.

(c) One clear advantage of the process is that the MPs in the House of Commons are democratically elected and this gives legitimacy to the decisions that they make. The process is thorough and allows important bills that deal with major issues of economic and social policy to receive adequate debate and scrutiny, particularly in committee, before they become law. The many stages through which a bill has to pass should ensure that all aspects have been considered thoroughly.

Another advantage is that if all the parties agree that a new law is needed urgently, the process is sufficiently flexible to allow this to happen. For example, the Criminal Justice (Terrorism and Conspiracy) Act 1998 went through all its stages in 2 days, and the Northern Ireland Bill 1972 was passed in just 24 hours.

It could also be argued that it is an advantage that the House of Lords, although unelected, is a check on the executive's powers, acting as a safeguard to the abuse of power by a government which, because of its large majority, is able to force through almost any law it wants. The Lords has made the government rethink its proposals to abolish jury trials in fraud cases, for example.

However, the role of the House of Lords could be seen as a significant restriction on the democratic process. The members of the House of Lords are not elected and this is seen as undemocratic, especially if they can prevent government-sponsored bills from being passed. While the Parliament Acts of 1911 and 1949 have restricted the power of the Lords to delaying rather than defeating a bill, in practice the Lords can often force the Commons to compromise rather than go through the process under the Parliament Acts. For example, in March 2005 the House of Lords forced the government to amend its plans in the Terrorism Bill for control orders to deal with terrorist suspects.

The process of statute creation can be slow and cumbersome, and this has the disadvantage of restricting the number of bills that can be passed. Inevitably, this means that measures that are not considered to be urgent or politically expedient do not get passed, for example the proposal to reform the law on non-fatal offences.

Finally, the government has a majority on all the standing committees and is able to defeat any amendments put forward in committee. As an extreme example, in the early 1990s the Conservative government's Water Privatisation Bill took up to 300 hours of parliamentary time spread over 3 months, and yet not one amendment of any substance emerged from either House.

> 🖉 There is sound recognition of the role of the House of Lords as a check on the government and the restrictions on its powers, and there is also mature discussion of other advantages and disadvantages. This answer clearly shows an understanding of the complexities of the process and an awareness of the fact that in some circumstances what has been presented as an advantage can be seen as a disadvantage. It would receive 10 marks.

Question 2

Delegated legislation

(a) Describe three types of delegated legislation.   (10 marks)

(b) Explain how delegated legislation is controlled by Parliament and
    the courts.   (10 marks)

(c) Discuss the effectiveness of these controls.   (10 marks)

■ ■ ■

A-grade answer

(a) Delegated legislation (secondary legislation) is legislation that is made not by Parliament but with its authority. Authority is given in an enabling Act, for example the Health and Safety at Work Act 1974 and the Court and Legal Services Act 1990.

Delegated legislation can take one of three forms, depending on the body that is authorised to make it. Orders in Council are made by the Privy Council. They are used when it would be inappropriate to use a statutory instrument, such as when transferring responsibilities between government departments. These were used to transfer powers from ministers in the UK government to the ministers in the devolved assembly in Scotland. If Parliament is not sitting and there is an emergency, the queen and Privy Council may make an Order in Council under the Emergency Powers Act 1920, as happened in the fuel crisis in 2000.

Statutory instruments take the form of rules, regulations and orders. Ministers and government departments are given the power to make statutory instruments relating to the jurisdiction of their ministry, for example the Minister of Transport has the power under various Road Traffic Acts to make detailed road traffic regulations. Regulations are a good way of updating primary legislation and adapting the law to changing circumstances. For example, the Health and Safety at Work Act 1974 was updated through the Management of Health and Safety at Work Regulations 1992. They apply to the whole country in their effect. Directives from the EU are also implemented in the form of statutory instruments, e.g. the Unfair Terms in Consumer Contracts Regulations.

The last form of delegated legislation is bylaws. These are made by local authorities, such as county or district councils. They are local in effect, only applying in the area of the council concerned, and are involved with such things as parking restrictions and activities that can or cannot be carried out in certain public places. Some public bodies such as British Rail can make bylaws to enforce rules covering behaviour in public places, e.g. the ban on smoking in the London Underground.

    ⒠ The answer shows clear understanding of the different types of delegated legislation, which is supported by relevant examples of each type and the bodies empowered to make them. The purpose of the enabling Act is explained and specific examples are given. All areas required are well covered and full marks would be awarded.

(b) Parliament has some limited control at the time the enabling Act is made, as it sets out the extent of the delegated powers in the Act. The Delegated Powers Scrutiny Committee in the House of Lords also looks at all legislation that delegates powers to see if they are inappropriate. All delegated legislation has to be laid before Parliament before it can come into force. Delegated legislation is subject to either an affirmative resolution, where both Houses of Parliament have to vote, approving the legislation within a certain time period; or a negative resolution, where the legislation is laid before Parliament and if no member puts down a motion to annul it within a specified period (40 days), it becomes law.

The Joint Committee on Statutory Instruments, a scrutiny committee composed of members from both Houses of Parliament, reviews all statutory instruments. It can draw Parliament's attention to any that need special consideration. If a statutory instrument imposes a tax, is defective, needs clarification or exceeds the powers granted in the Act, it will be referred back to Parliament. Parliament itself holds the ultimate safeguard because it can withdraw the delegated powers and revoke a piece of delegated legislation at any time.

✍ All aspects of the controls that Parliament has over delegated legislation are well covered.

Delegated legislation can be challenged in the courts. Any person who has a personal interest in the delegated legislation (i.e. is affected by it) may apply to the court under the judicial review procedure. This is on the grounds that the delegated legislation is *ultra vires*, it goes beyond the powers granted by Parliament. This can be in the form of either procedural *ultra vires*, where a public authority has not followed the proper procedure set out in the enabling Act (as in *Agricultural, Horticultural and Forestry Training Board* v *Aylesbury Mushrooms Ltd*, where the ministry failed to consult the interested parties) or substantive *ultra vires*, where the delegated legislation exceeds the powers in the enabling Act. In *R* v *Home Secretary ex parte Fire Brigades Union* (1995), where the home secretary made changes to the Criminal Injuries Compensation Scheme, he was held to have exceeded the power given in the Criminal Justice Act 1988. Another example is *R* v *Secretary of State for Education ex parte National Union of Teachers*. The High Court decided that rules for teachers' appraisal went beyond powers given in the Education Act 1996.

✍ The grounds for judicial review are explained well, with both procedural and substantive *ultra vires* covered in detail. Relevant cases are given in support. This answer would receive 10 marks.

(c) The controls by Parliament have drawbacks. One major problem is the fact that there are over 3,000 statutory instruments made each year. This has the effect that some pieces of legislation which may not be suitable may slip through the review procedure. The affirmative procedure does draw Parliament's attention to the delegated legislation, but it is only possible on rare occasions to prevent the legislation from being passed. The committee in the House of Lords has limited powers. Although it reports to the House of Lords before the committee stage, it has no power to amend the bill. The Scrutiny Committee is more important and has had some success in having changes made to some pieces of delegated legislation. It lacks power because it can only consider whether the delegated powers have been used properly, and not the merits of the legislation. Its reports are not binding.

Control by the courts has been more successful, with many challenges being upheld, e.g. the decisions in *R v Home Secretary ex parte Fire Brigades Union* (1995) and *R v Secretary of State for Education ex parte National Union of Teachers*. However, using the courts has problems. It relies on individuals or other bodies who are affected by the legislation bringing a case to court. This can be a costly and time-consuming business. Significantly perhaps, the two cases referred to above were brought by trade unions rather than individuals. It is doubtful whether many individuals would have had the resources to bring judicial review proceedings in the High Court. Also, the delegated legislation may be in force for years before it is challenged, and the discretionary powers, conferred on the minister under the Act, may be extremely wide, making it difficult to establish that he or she has acted *ultra vires*.

Despite these problems, it is important to have controls over delegated legislation and they have been shown to work in some instances, which is better than having no controls at all. Also Parliament does have the power to repeal the enabling Act, which is an important safeguard.

Although fairly brief, this answer identifies relevant issues concerning the control of delegated legislation and attempts a genuine discussion, with both positive and negative points and a conclusion. It would receive 10 marks.

Question 3

Statutory interpretation

(a) **Briefly describe two external aids which judges can use to interpret Acts of Parliament.** (10 marks)

(b) **Describe two rules or approaches to statutory interpretation which can help judges to interpret statutes.** (10 marks)

(c) **Briefly describe the advantages and disadvantages of one of the rules of statutory interpretation.** (10 marks)

■ ■ ■

A-grade answer

(a) External aids are those outside the Act itself. Dictionaries of various kinds are the most obvious external aid and they are used frequently as a means of discovering what words mean. For example in *Vaughan* v *Vaughan* (1973), where a man had been pestering his ex-wife, the Court of Appeal used a dictionary in order to define 'molest' and concluded that the definition was wide enough to cover his behaviour. However, the use of dictionaries does not always produce unanimity. In *Coltman* v *Bibby Tankers* (1987), reference to dictionaries did not result in unanimous views on whether the word 'equipment' could include a ship. The majority in the Court of Appeal, referring to the *Oxford English Dictionary*, said that it could not, whereas Lord Oliver in the House of Lords said that there was nothing in the *OED* definition that prevented a ship being included.

A second external aid is *Hansard*, the official report of what is said in Parliament. In *Davis* v *Johnson*, Lord Denning argued that not to refer to *Hansard* was like groping around in the dark without putting the light on. The House of Lords initially rejected Lord Denning's view, but it was eventually accepted by the Lords, subject to strict conditions, in *Pepper* v *Hart* (1993). *Pepper* v *Hart* overruled *Davis* v *Johnson* and allowed reference to *Hansard* when wording in a statute is ambiguous, obscure or leads to an absurdity; when the material relied upon consists of one or more statements by a minister or other promoter of the bill, together if necessary with such other parliamentary material as is required to understand such statements and their effect; and when the statements relied upon are clear.

Recent cases have suggested that the courts may limit the use of *Pepper* v *Hart* to those cases against the government. Lord Hope said in *R* v *A* (2001) that essentially reference to *Hansard* 'is available for the purpose only of *preventing* the executive from placing a different meaning on words used in legislation from that which they attributed to those words when promoting the legislation in Parliament'.

When dealing with cases involving Acts that have introduced into English law an international convention or European directive, a wider use of *Hansard* is permitted. It was held in *Three Rivers DC* v *Bank of England* (1996) that the *Pepper* v *Hart* principle did not have to be applied so narrowly because it was important to construe the statute purposively and consistently with any European materials like directives.

🖉 This answer makes detailed comments about both the aids selected and uses relevant cases to illustrate effectively the way the aids work in practice. It would receive 10 marks.

(b) The literal rule involves giving words their plain, ordinary, dictionary meaning. Lord Reid in *Pinner* v *Everett* referred to 'the natural and ordinary meaning of that word or phrase in its context'.

The literal rule was used in *Whiteley* v *Chappell* (1868). A statute made it an offence to 'impersonate any person entitled to vote' in an election. The defendant impersonated a dead person, and applying the literal rule, a dead person is not entitled to vote in an election. It was also used in *London and North Eastern Railway Co.* v *Berriman* (1946), where Mrs Berriman was unable to obtain any compensation because her husband was killed while carrying out maintenance work (oiling points) on the railway line and not 'relaying or repairing' it.

It was also used in *Cutter* v *Eagle Star Insurance Co.* (1998), in which the House of Lords decided that the word 'road' in the Road Traffic Act 1988 could not include a car park. The issue was significant because the insurance company would only have to pay compensation if a car was parked on a road.

The golden rule is really a subsidiary of the literal rule. It states that judges should use the literal rule unless it would produce an absurdity.

Under the narrow application, proposed by Lord Reid in *Jones* v *DPP* (1962), if a word is ambiguous the judge may choose between possible meanings of the word in order to avoid an absurd outcome. For example, in *R* v *Allen* (1872) the issue was that s.57 of the Offences Against the Person Act 1861 made it an offence to 'marry' if you were already married. The court decided that 'marry' could have two meanings — to become legally married and to go through a ceremony of marriage. It would clearly be absurd to apply the first meaning, because no one could then be convicted of bigamy.

The wider application is where there is only one meaning but this would lead to an absurd or repugnant situation, and for policy reasons this would be unacceptable. A clear example is *Re Sigsworth* (1935). Under the Administration of Estates Act 1925, the property of a person who died without making a will would pass to his or her next of kin. In this case, Sigsworth had murdered his mother, and it was clearly repugnant that a person who murdered his mother could then under the provisions of a statute inherit her property.

Another example is *Adler* v *George* (1964), where it was clearly both repugnant and absurd that the offence could be committed by causing an obstruction in the vicinity of a prohibited place but not within the place itself.

✐ This answer explains the two rules clearly and gives examples to support the description. The whole response is thorough and uses cases both to define the rules and to illustate how they work. It would be awarded 10 marks.

(c) The mischief rule is regarded by most modern commentators as the best of the three rules, because it tries to give effect to the true intention of Parliament.

One advantage is that it allows judges, in Lord Denning's words, to 'fill in the gaps' when Parliament has left something out and to use common sense and change wording to reflect the problem that the Act was trying to deal with. *Smith* v *Hughes* could be seen as a sensible decision, reflecting what Parliament would have done had it been able to anticipate the situation.

Another advantage is that it allows judges to interpret statutes in the light of changing social, economic and technological circumstances. A good example is the decision of the House of Lords in *Royal College of Nursing* v *DHSS*, which recognised that medical practice had changed since the passing of the Abortion Act because of the development of new techniques.

A disadvantage of the mischief rule is that finding the intention of Parliament is not easy, even if *Hansard* is used; and by restricting the use of *Hansard* to statements by ministers, there is the danger that it will reveal the intention of the government but not necessarily the intention of Parliament.

The mischief rule also gives too much power to judges. It could be argued that it should be Parliament that makes any changes. It is not right that judges should try to second-guess what Parliament meant. Lord Denning's argument in *Magor and St Mellons* that judges should look for the intention of Parliament, even when there was no ambiguity, was criticised by Viscount Simonds as 'a naked usurpation of the legislative function under the thin disguise of interpretation'. Lord Scarman commented that 'if Parliament says one thing but means another, it is not...for the courts to correct it.... We are to be governed not by Parliament's intentions, but by Parliament's enactments'.

✐ This response discusses both advantages and disadvantages of the mischief rule in detail and would receive full marks. The comments are perceptive and supported by relevant authorities. The cases are used to back up the arguments, but time is not wasted outlining the facts.

Question 4

Precedent

(a) Briefly explain the main features of precedent. (10 marks)

(b) Describe how judges can avoid precedent. (10 marks)

(c) Discuss the advantages and disadvantages of being able to avoid precedent. (10 marks)

■ ■ ■

A-grade answer

(a) The first element of precedent is *ratio decidendi* ('the reason for deciding'), which is the judge's written judgement setting out the facts and the legal principles used to reach the decision. The *ratio* forms the binding precedent to be followed in later cases. An example of *ratio decidendi* is the rule in *R* v *Nedrick* (1986), confirmed in *R* v *Woollin* (1997), that if a jury considers that the defendant foresaw death or serious injury as a virtual certainty, oblique intention may be inferred. Another example is the judgement in *R* v *Cunningham* (1957) that to be reckless you have to know there is a risk of the unlawful consequence and decide to take the risk.

Not all of the legal principles form the binding precedent. Sometimes a judge will state what he or she thinks the law would be if the facts were slightly different. This is known as *obiter dicta* and can form persuasive precedent. This happened in *R* v *Howe,* which was a murder case. The House of Lords commented that duress was not a valid defence (*ratio*), but it also said that it would not be a defence to someone charged with attempted murder either (*obiter*). Persuasive precedent may also result from dissenting judgements, when a case is decided by a majority of judges, or from decisions of the Privy Council as in the *Wagon Mound* case (the principle of remoteness of damage in tort).

To make sure that judicial precedent works, a court hierarchy has developed whereby the lower courts are bound by the decisions of the ones above them. The highest court is the House of Lords (HL). All the other courts in England have to follow its decisions, but the Practice Statement 1966 allows it to depart from its own previous decisions when it appears right to do so. For example, *Pepper* v *Hart* (1993) overruled the previous House of Lords ruling in *Davis* v *Johnson*, which banned the use of *Hansard* in statutory interpretation.

The Court of Appeal (CA) is bound to follow the decisions of the HL. The Civil Division is also bound to follow its own previous decisions, unless the exceptions in *Young* v *Bristol Aeroplane Co. Ltd* (1944) apply. The Criminal Division is bound by its own previous decisions, with the exceptions listed in *Young*, and also if someone's liberty is at stake (*R* v *Spencer* 1985) or to ensure justice (*R* v *Simpson* 2003).

The High Court is bound by the HL and the CA. The Crown Court, County Court and

Magistrates' Court are all bound by the decisions of the courts above them. They are not bound by their own previous decisions.

With so many cases being heard every year, there has to be some way in which the lawyers/judges can find out which decisions they must follow. To make sure that this is achieved, a comprehensive system of law reporting has been established. In every case that is decided in the courts which set the precedents, the judgement is written down and published in these reports, e.g. the All England Law Reports, the Weekly Law Reports.

> An accurate explanation of the hierarchy of the courts is crucial when answering a question on how precedent works, as is a description of *ratio decidendi*. For the higher marks, it is not sufficient merely to identify and define it — there must be some explanation with case material in support. As precedent is based on decided cases, the use of cases is essential in the answer. Another important feature that is often overlooked is the necessity for a system of law reporting. This answer would receive 10 marks.

(b) The courts may be able to distinguish the present case from that in which the precedent was set; if the judge finds that the facts of the cases are sufficiently different, he or she can avoid following precedent. The Court of Appeal used this method in *Boardman* v *Sanderson* (1964), where it was able to depart from the decision in *King* v *Phillips* (1953). In both cases, the parent of a child had heard screams when their child's bicycle was run over by a car. Neither parent saw the accident but both claimed they had suffered nervous shock. The claim failed in the first case as the child was not injured, but succeeded in the second case because the child was injured.

Judges in the higher courts can overrule the decisions of the lower courts if they decide that the legal principles are wrong. The 1966 Practice Statement in the House of Lords allows the court to depart from its own previous decisions where it is right to do so. This means that it can avoid following precedent, but it has only done so on a few occasions. In *Pepper* v *Hart* it overruled its decision in *Davis* v *Johnson* that judges could not refer to *Hansard* when interpreting a statute. *R* v *Shivpuri* (1986) was the first criminal case in which the power under the Practice Statement was used. The House of Lords overruled its decision in *Anderton* v *Ryan* made just a few months earlier.

Reversing is where a higher court overrules a lower court in the same case. A good example of this is the case of *Gillick*. In the High Court, the case was decided against Mrs Gillick. She appealed and the Court of Appeal reversed the decision. The Area Health Authority then appealed and the House of Lords reversed the decision again. Another example is *Sweet* v *Parsley*. The defendant was convicted in the Magistrates' Court, her conviction was upheld in the divisional court and then reversed by the House of Lords.

> This is another answer where the use of cases is important to illustrate how the methods work. A few are used here, but you should be able to use the cases you have come across, during your study of Unit 1 and wider reading, to enhance your

answer. To secure a good mark, you must cover several methods of avoiding precedent, as this answer does. It would receive full marks.

(c) One advantage of being able to avoid precedent is that judges can develop the law. There are several aspects to this. First, it prevents Parliament from having to legislate and means that changes can occur naturally when a suitable case comes before the courts, rather than many months or even years later when Parliament considers the matter. A good example is the case of *British Railways Board* v *Herrington,* which was one of the first cases to make use of the Practice Statement allowing the House of Lords to overrule its own earlier decisions and which established the principle that a duty of care could be owed to a trespasser in certain circumstances.

Another advantage is that judges, by avoiding precedent, can achieve justice in individual cases. Arguably, this was the case in *Merritt* v *Merritt* (1970), where the defendant husband sought to rely on the principle in *Balfour* v *Balfour* (1919) that a wife was unable to enforce a maintenance agreement made with her husband, in order that he could avoid honouring an agreement he had made with his estranged wife. The court distinguished the case on the basis that the agreement, albeit made within marriage, had been made after the couple had separated.

A further advantage is that avoiding precedent occurs in a controlled way. The Practice Statement does not apply to the Court of Appeal, and this greatly restricts the number of cases to which it can apply. Also the House of Lords has used its powers with restraint, and to date they have been applied less than 50 times in the 40 years during which it has had this freedom.

However, there are also disadvantages. First, there will be uncertainty in the law. One of the strengths of precedent is that it enables lawyers to advise their clients with some confidence, knowing that the law has been clearly confirmed in a previous case. It is unhelpful to have a legal principle reversed when people have acted on the understanding that the law was clear. The decision in *Murphy* v *Brentwood District Council* (1990) to overrule *Anns* v *Merton London Borough Council* (1977) on the duty of care owed by local authorities when approving building plans significantly altered the degree of protection purchasers of properties thought they enjoyed.

A further disadvantage is that judges will make artificial distinctions in order to avoid a precedent. In *Rickards* v *Lothian,* the House of Lords decided to interpret the requirement in *Rylands* v *Fletcher* that something should be brought onto land for a 'non-natural purpose' as meaning non-natural in a social sense, so that piped water became 'natural'. It seems quite evident that this was an artificial distinction, designed to avoid following the precedent.

📝 This question is not asking about the advantages and disadvantages of precedent, but about the advantages and disadvantages of being able to avoid precedent, although some of the arguments used here would also be relevant in a question on the merits of precedent. Notice that the points are developed and not simply stated in a single sentence. They are also supported by a range of cases. The answer would be awarded 10 marks.

Section B

Question 1

Juries (I)

(a) Describe the selection of juries for Crown Court trials. (10 marks)

(b) Explain the function of a jury in criminal trials. (10 marks)

■ ■ ■

A-grade answer

(a) The criteria for the selection of juries are laid down in the Juries Act 1974, which requires jurors to be aged 18–70 (the Criminal Justice Act 1988 increased age eligibility to 70 from 65), to be on the electoral register and to have been resident in the UK (including the Channel Islands and the Isle of Man) for 5 years from the age of 13. Jurors are summoned by random sampling carried out initially by the Central Jury Summoning Bureau. From the number summoned for jury service, after excusal or deferral the clerk will randomly select 20 as 'jurors in waiting', then the final 12 jurors are chosen.

There are, however, certain people who are either disqualified from, or ineligible for, jury service. Those with a serious criminal record who have served a prison sentence within the previous 10 years or who have served any community sentence within the previous 5 years are disqualified. Under the Criminal Justice Act 2003, only the mentally ill are ineligible. Judges, lawyers and police officers are now eligible for jury service. Only those over 65 may be excused from jury service as of right. Some people may be excused at the discretion of the court, e.g. nursing mothers, students sitting public exams or those with a poor command of English, but most such people are now likely to have jury service deferred until a later date.

Jurors may be vetted and challenged. Peremptory challenge by the defence (i.e. challenging without cause) was ended by the Criminal Justice Act 1988. Defence may now only challenge a juror with cause. The prosecution may require a juror to 'Stand by for the Crown', but this is rarely employed and it is usual for a reason to be given. More detailed checks on a juror's background may only be carried out with the approval of the Attorney General, and this will be given only in security or terrorist trials.

> All the relevant materials — statutory criteria for jury service, random selection, the major changes introduced under the Criminal Justice Act 2003 — are included in this answer. Although only worth 10 marks, the answer should still cover the issues of challenges and vetting, which this response does succinctly. This answer would receive 10 marks.

(b) The function of a jury in a criminal trial in Crown Courts is to decide the issue of guilt or innocence of the defendant. The jury acts as 'master of the facts', whereas the judge is 'master of the law'. The jury hears all the evidence in the trial, provided by both the prosecution and the defence. Jurors are encouraged to take notes and may ask questions of any witness through the judge.

At the end of the trial, after closing speeches by counsel, the judge sums up the evidence and directs the jury on all relevant points of law. In a complicated trial, the judge may provide the jury with a series of questions to assist its deliberations. The jurors retire to a room where, in strict privacy, they consider their verdict. A foreman is selected to speak for the jury and should lead the jurors in their discussions.

If after 2 hours 10 minutes the jurors have not reached a unanimous verdict, the judge may recall them to advise that a majority verdict upon which at least ten are agreed will be accepted — this was first provided by the Criminal Justice Act 1967. Only about one fifth of all verdicts are by a majority.

When a verdict has been decided, the jury returns to court and the foreman delivers the verdict to the judge.

> Note how detailed the description of the role and functions of the jury is. Too often candidates simply write that it is the role of a jury to bring in a verdict of 'guilty' or 'not guilty', without attempting to explain *how* juries perform their task. Full marks would be awarded for this response.

■ ■ ■

C-grade answer

(a) A jury is a group of unqualified citizens who take part in the English legal system. It will be randomly selected from the electoral register by a computer. To serve on a jury, a person has to be aged from 18 to 70, be on the electoral register and have lived in the UK for at least 5 years from the age of 13 (Juries Act 1974).

There are a number of reasons why people may not be able to serve on a jury: if they have committed a serious offence within the previous 10 years, if they suffer from a mental illness or have a poor command of English. Under the Criminal Justice Act 2004, those involved in the administration of justice are now eligible for jury service.

A person may be excused from jury service if aged between 65 and 70 years. Once it has been decided whether a person may sit, he or she arrives at court and will normally sit for a period of 2 weeks. Twenty names are put into a hat and then 12 are selected to be sworn in as the jury.

> The comparison between this answer and the A-grade answer above is obvious. There are weak statutory references, and a particular problem is the 'grouping' of the categories of ineligibility, disqualification and excusal. This answer would receive 7 marks.

Question 2

Juries (II)

(a) Explain and evaluate the advantages of the use of juries in criminal cases. **(10 marks)**

(b) Explain and evaluate the disadvantages of the use of juries in criminal cases. **(10 marks)**

■ ■ ■

A-grade answer

(a) First of all, juries only feature in about 1% of all criminal trials — 97% of all criminal cases are dealt with in Magistrates' Courts. However, juries continue to play an important role in our system of criminal justice. Juries allow the ordinary citizen to play a significant part in the administration of justice. This means that verdicts can be viewed as those of society rather than exclusively those of professional lawyers and judges.

It has long been argued that the right to be tried by your peers is a bastion of liberty against the state. This was well demonstrated in *R* v *Ponting*, where a senior civil servant at the Ministry of Defence was charged under the Official Secrets Act with unlawfully passing secret material to an MP. He was legally guilty, but the jury acquitted him, believing that his prosecution was politically inspired and no harm had in fact been done to national security.

Trial by jury is over 1,000 years old and this tradition is held in high esteem. This is confirmed by the controversy that arises whenever governments propose to limit jury trial, especially in fraud cases.

One of the principal arguments for trial by jury is that of 'layman's equity' — the power that juries, unlike judges or magistrates, have to return a verdict of 'not guilty' even where in strict law it is clear that the defendant is guilty, but in the circumstances the jury considers that a conviction would not be fair. This happened in *R* v *Owen*, where a man who shot and injured the man who had killed his 11-year-old son in a serious traffic accident was acquitted.

Juries have been subjected to considerable criticism in recent years in terms of their alleged lack of competence, high acquittal rates (when compared to those of Magistrates' Courts) and the cost of jury trials. The issue of competence has arisen specifically with reference to complex fraud trials, which can last many months. It is argued that the highly technical details that are introduced in evidence in such trials cannot be understood by jurors. However, after the collapse of the Jubilee Line fraud case, research concluded that 'a better monument to the endeavours of juries in this country or a better justification for the jury system would be hard to find'.

In any considered evaluation, it is hard to escape the conclusion that, while it is clear that improvements can be made to jury trials, juries have become an entrenched part of our criminal justice system, and without juries public confidence would diminish. It also remains true that as Lord Devlin once famously stated, 'juries are the lamp that shows that freedom lives'.

More than for any other topic, answers about advantages (and disadvantages) of juries in criminal cases tend to be written in simplistic terms and rely on bulleted lists. However, this response avoids these traps and gives a full and detailed explanation of the key advantages of juries, developing the argument of 'layman's equity' with case examples as support. The answer then addresses one of the major arguments against juries — their alleged inability to deal with complex fraud trials. The assertion is analysed critically, with reference to the Jubilee Line case. This answer would receive 10 marks.

(b) One of the most serious criticisms concerning juries is the high acquittal rate when compared to trials in Magistrates' Courts. However, such a comparison is not helpful, since the nature of summary cases is usually much more 'fact-based' and the great majority of defendants plead guilty. One factor leading to higher acquittal rates has been said to be the large number of middle-class, professional people who are able to evade jury service through ineligibility or excusal. One of the key sections in the Criminal Justice Act 2003 was the elimination of such categories, and this has led to more representative juries.

A further criticism is that jury trials are much more expensive than summary trials, but this criticism is misplaced. The major costs of Crown Court trials are those of professional judges, lawyers, expert witnesses etc. The average jury cost does not exceed £1,000.

The argument that juries have insufficient competence to deal with fraud cases was undermined by the research into the Jubilee Line case, which confirmed that the jury in that case fully understood the complex issues.

Finally, there remains the serious issue of 'jury nobbling', whereby jurors are intimidated or bribed to acquit defendants. In order to protect jurors, the Metropolitan Police Force spends up to £4.5 million per year. Additional protection against nobbling was also introduced in the Criminal Procedure and Investigation Act 1996, which allows the retrial of a defendant acquitted as a result of jury nobbling. While this is a major problem, it cannot by itself even begin to justify the removal of juries from serous criminal trials in the UK.

This is another well-argued answer, which avoids the temptation simply to list points. It successfully challenges some of the criticisms that have been directed against juries. The particular issue of jury nobbling is explained clearly, but it is then argued this does not justify the ending of jury trials. This answer would also receive 10 marks.

C-grade answer

(a) The main advantage of juries is that 12 people making a decision are better than one. This is because it is more likely to eliminate any bias. Another advantage is that jurors are lay people and are therefore unqualified in law. This means that they should have a more objective view of the case than a lawyer or judge. The jury will also balance out the number of legal professionals.

Another advantage is that of 'layman's equity', where juries can 'bend' the law in order to give a 'just' verdict in some cases, e.g. *R* v *Owen*.

🖉 This is a much weaker answer that simply makes assertions, rather than providing reasoned arguments. It would receive 4–5 marks.

(b) A big disadvantage of using a jury is that it may not understand everything it hears in court — this can be a particular problem when hearing long and complicated fraud trials. This could mean that jurors will be unable to make a fair and just decision. A further disadvantage of juries is their cost — Crown Court trials are much more expensive than trials in Magistrates' Courts.

However, it can also be argued that juries are not entirely free from pressures, as 'jury nobbling' occurs in a number of serious trials such as the Brinks-Mat gold robbery trial, and the protection of jurors in such cases is extremely expensive.

🖉 This is a typical C-/D-grade answer to this question; the points are mentioned rather than explained or analysed. The issue of juries' ability to try fraud trials is insufficiently examined when compared to the A-grade answer above. The idea of 'jury nobbling' is not explained, and the answer fails to mention that since the advent of majority verdicts in the Criminal Justice Act 1967, this problem has become far less serious. This answer would receive 4–5 marks.

Question 3

Magistrates (I)

(a) Outline the criminal jurisdiction of magistrates within the English legal system.
(10 marks)

(b) Briefly consider the advantages and disadvantages of magistrates within the English legal system.
(10 marks)

■ ■ ■

A-grade answer

(a) Magistrates play by far the largest role in the criminal justice system as they try about 97% of all criminal trials — all summary offences and most either-way offences. For either-way offences, there will be a preliminary hearing called 'plea before venue', where the accused person is given the choice of summary trial by magistrates or trial before judge and jury in the Crown Court. Sentencing powers of magistrates in adult courts are a maximum fine of £5,000 and/or a prison sentence of 6 months.

Magistrates also try most offences committed by young offenders (aged 10–17), in the youth court. The only offence that cannot be tried here is murder. The youth court is less formal than the adult court and magistrates must have received additional training to carry out this work. The maximum sentence available in this court is a 2-year training and detention order.

Other functions within the criminal justice system include bail applications (under the Bail Act 1976), applications for legal aid, and the issue of search and arrest warrants.

Finally, lay magistrates continue to sit with a circuit judge in appeals to the Crown Court against conviction.

📝 This is a brief but accurate description of the criminal jurisdiction of magistrates, in which the key responsibilities of adult courts — summary and either-way offences — and youth courts are dealt with effectively. Mention is made of the other duties — bail and legal aid applications, warrants and dealing with appeals. This answer would obtain 10 marks.

(b) Magistrates have historically been an important part of the criminal justice system for more than 1,000 years, and they enable members of the community to become involved in the administration of criminal justice. They are the most representative type of judges — unlike our professional judiciary, almost 50% are women with almost 8.5% drawn from ethnic minorities. They also provide 'local' justice, as they have to live within a short distance of their bench; this gives them a greater awareness of local events and local patterns of crime.

Because magistrates are unpaid, Magistrates' Courts are the only 'profit-making' component of the criminal justice system, as the value of fines exceeds the overall costs of these courts. They are also much quicker in bringing cases to trial than is the case with Crown Courts, where delays of up to a year are not uncommon.

The most significant disadvantage of magistrates is the serious level of inconsistency in their sentencing. Surveys continue to show that some benches are ten times more likely to impose custodial sentences than neighbouring benches. This is clearly unfair — simple justice demands that similar offenders receive broadly similar sentences.

It is also argued that because magistrates are not legally qualified, this justice is 'amateur justice'. This fails to take into consideration the fact that magistrates are now selected far more carefully and receive much more detailed training under the Magistrates National Training Initiative (MNTI 2) than was the case several years ago. Furthermore, the importance of the partnership that magistrates form with a legally qualified clerk needs to be noted. The overall success of Magistrates' Courts is, however, confirmed by the low 'success' rate of appeals against both sentence and conviction.

This answer contains a fully argued appraisal of the advantages and disadvantages of magistrates. The key point to note here is that this is not simply a list of each, but a careful consideration of the various issues. There is a vast difference between writing 'magistrates can be criticised because they are not legally qualified' and writing the content of the last paragraph. The answer would score 9 or 10 marks.

Question 4

Magistrates (II)

Describe how magistrates are appointed. (10 marks)

■ ■ ■

A-grade answer

In order to become a magistrate, a person can either apply to the local advisory committee, which exists for every bench, or be nominated by local political parties or voluntary bodies. The statutory qualifications are that the applicant must be under the age of 65 and live or work within a short distance of the court within which he or she will normally be working. Although until recently applicants had to be 27 years old to be appointed, this is no longer a requirement, and some candidates as young as 19 have been appointed. Successful candidates are required to spend an average of half a day per week sitting in court. The current procedures for selection and appointment are contained within the Justices of the Peace Act 1979.

Categories of people who are excluded from appointment include police officers, members of the armed forces, undischarged bankrupts and those who have a serious criminal record.

After application or nomination, references are checked, as is the person's criminal record. A shortlist is drawn up by the committee and two interviews are held: the first measures the candidate's general character; the second, which comprises a number of judging and sentencing exercises, assesses the candidate's judgement. After all the candidates have been interviewed, the committee meets to consider the various issues of balance. The Lord Chancellor has made it clear that he requires broadly equal numbers of men and women, and a wide spread of occupation, ethnic origin and, to a lesser extent, political affiliation and age. The committee will finally recommend names to the Lord Chancellor, who usually accepts these recommendations and will formally appoint the magistrates. At the conclusion of the selection and appointment procedure, successful candidates are formally sworn in as magistrates at a ceremony conducted by a senior circuit judge.

Before sitting in court, newly appointed magistrates are required to attend an extensive training and mentoring programme organised by the Judicial Studies Board — the Magistrates New Training Initiative 2.

   ✍ This answer is well planned and developed. The facts are set out and explained clearly, and there is a sound sequence to the factual material. The qualifications are described first, then the reasons for disqualification, followed by the selection procedures, including the two interviews and the need for a balanced bench. The role of the Lord Chancellor is explained accurately, and the conclusion to this process is presented neatly — the swearing-in of the new magistrates with a brief reference to their training and mentoring programme. This answer would receive the full 10 marks.

■ ■ ■

C-/D-grade answer

Anyone wishing to become a lay magistrate must apply to a local advisory committee. They can be recommended by anyone, including themselves, but more often it is by local trade unions or political parties. The job of the advisory committee is to decide who is suitable for the job and pass on their names to the Lord Chancellor, who can then appoint those people as magistrates in their local commission area.

No formal qualifications in law are required. However, magistrates must live locally to the court on which they are to sit and be under the age of 65 on appointment. Anyone who is a police officer or a traffic warden is disqualified, as are those with a serious criminal record. The selection procedure involves checking candidates' references and then conducting two interviews with shortlisted candidates.

Once appointed, they will receive appropriate training and mentoring, and are then supposed to sit about 35 times a year.

This answer is much weaker than the A-grade answer. There is no reference to statutory requirements. Although quite good on the issue of basic qualifications and those disqualified, this answer comes across as lacking authority. The answer would score just 5 marks.

Question 5

Legal professions (I)

(a) Outline the qualifications and training required to become a
 barrister and a solicitor. (10 marks)
(b) Briefly describe the work carried out by both solicitors and barristers.
(10 marks)

■ ■ ■

A-grade answer

(a) In order to become a solicitor, most people take a university degree, not necessarily
in law. If another degree is taken, or a non-qualifying law degree, a further year's
study is taken to pass the Graduate Diploma in Law (GDL), formerly the Common
Professional Examination (CPE). The next part of the qualifying course is the Legal
Practice Course (LPC), which is a 1-year, full-time course (or takes 2 years part
time). Finally, students have to obtain a training contract in a solicitors' firm, which
lasts 2 years.

After the successful completion of the traineeship, the trainee will be admitted as a
solicitor by the Law Society and his or her name will be added to the roll of solicitors. It is also possible for mature entrants to qualify as solicitors by first qualifying
as legal executives and then as Fellows of ILEX, after which they take the LPC or the
2-year traineeship. Even after qualification, solicitors are required to attend specialised training courses as part of their continuing professional development.

Entry to the Bar is for graduates only — but it is not essential for the student to have
studied law. If the degree is in another subject (or a non-qualifying law degree), the
GDL has to be taken. After graduation or completion of the GDL, students have to
apply to an Inn of Court and be accepted on the Bar Vocational Course (BVC). If
these exams are passed and the required number of dinners have been taken, the
student is admitted to the Bar by his or her Inn of Court. Students need to obtain a
pupillage in a set of chambers, which lasts one more year. This work involves 'shad-
owing' a barrister, who acts as pupil-master. During this period, students must also
follow a programme of continuing professional education organised by the Bar
Council. On completion of pupillage, the barrister needs to find a tenancy in a set of
chambers in order to practise as an independent barrister.

 📝 All relevant details — *in the correct order* — are provided in this answer, which
 would obtain the full 10 marks. Students should note the inclusion of the ILEX
 route to becoming a solicitor.

(b) The work of solicitors is largely non-litigious, although they do have rights of audience in both County and Magistrates' Courts. Their work involves conveyancing

(transferring property rights) and probate (wills and executory work), together with giving general legal advice to clients, which could include family law, employment law or setting up companies etc. Under the Courts and Legal Services Act 1990 (as amended by the Access to Justice Act 1999), solicitors can acquire higher-court rights of audience by qualifying as solicitor-advocates — there are at present about 2,000 of these. Most solicitors work within a partnership with other solicitors. Over recent years, in both London and large cities, there has been a trend for law firms to merge to create much larger partnerships, which in turn has led to greater specialisation in the work undertaken by solicitors.

The Bar is a referral profession, i.e. clients have to see a solicitor first (unless they are members of another profession, e.g. accountants, in which case there is direct professional access), although Direct Public Access is now available for certain kinds of case. Barristers are self-employed and usually work from a set of chambers where they share administrative and secretarial expenses with other barristers. The majority of barristers concentrate on advocacy, representing clients in court, but they also provide specialist advice through counsel's opinions to solicitors. The litigation work of a barrister also includes drafting pleadings prior to the case coming to court. Barristers have rights of audience in all English courts.

🖉 This is a well-balanced answer in which the functions of each professional are described fully and clearly. Use of specialised legal language is accurate and there is appropriate statutory reference. The work of solicitors is explained well — usually, candidates fail to distinguish between the non-litigious work and the court work undertaken by solicitors. The key strength of this essay lies in its balanced plan; its structure addresses all the issues raised in the question. It would receive the full 10 marks.

Question 6

Legal professions (II)

Outline recent changes to the legal profession and comment briefly on the suggestion that it is no longer necessary for there to be two distinct professions of solicitor and barrister.

(10 marks)

■ ■ ■

A-grade answer

During the last two decades, there have been many changes to the legal profession. Solicitors lost their monopoly over conveyancing, but under the Courts and Legal Services Act (CLSA) 1990 they obtained higher-court rights of audience as solicitor-advocates, and there are now over 2,000 of these. Other changes have seen solicitors become High Court judges and the growth of large, even multinational, firms of solicitors, which has led to increasing specialisation within law firms.

Barristers, too, have seen many changes within their profession. They can now advertise their services, and professional clients can consult directly with barristers. Direct Public Access now permits ordinary members of the public to obtain advice from barristers, but only in civil law matters. Sets of chambers have merged in recent years, reflecting the trend with solicitors.

These are just a few of the changes that have occurred recently. In the Access to Justice Act 1999, employed barristers acquired rights of audience for the first time, and the Act made it easier for solicitors to obtain higher-court rights of audience.

Because of these changes, especially the opportunity for solicitors to advocate in the higher courts and to become senior judges, the question has been raised as to whether it is necessary to have two separate branches of the legal profession. The UK is the only developed country where there are two different professions. In other European countries and in the USA, there is only one 'fused' profession, where lawyers specialise in either court- or office-based work, but they receive a common training and are governed by the same professional body.

However, to answer this question, it is also essential to consider the very different tasks that each branch — solicitors and barristers — performs. For most of us, the only time we see a solicitor is when we are buying or selling our house or making a will. It is rare for such 'administrative' tasks to require a referral to a specialist barrister to obtain counsel's opinion.

If a decision is taken by a client to pursue or defend a case in court, the solicitor will instruct a barrister or solicitor-advocate to represent the client. In such circumstances, it is necessary also to appreciate that while the barrister may be the courtroom specialist advocate, the solicitor, too, is a specialist — in issuing the proceedings in court to start the action and dealing with the pre-action protocols such as discovery and organising witness statements. The process of litigation has to involve both solicitors and barristers.

Given that most people's legal problems can be and are dealt with successfully by solicitors, and that on the relatively rare occasions where court action is necessary both 'office-based' and 'court-based' lawyers are used, it seems unarguable that the public interest is best served by having two separate sets of lawyers.

> This question creates many problems for candidates. It illustrates the need for detailed planning, as candidates are required first of all to identify various changes that have affected both solicitors and barristers, and only then should they discuss whether two separate legal professions are needed.
>
> The key to answering the second part of this question lies in understanding the relationship that exists between solicitors and barristers. Too often students appear to learn only the differences that exist between the two branches without appreciating the way in which they work together. A particular problem is that too many students fail to realise how much legal work is non-contentious (such as conveyancing) or how much litigious work solicitors perform themselves in Magistrates' and County Courts, and, finally, that even where a barrister is instructed there is still much specialised work to be undertaken by the solicitor. All these points are covered well in this answer, and it would accordingly receive 10 marks.

■ ■ ■

C-/D-grade answer

Due to the passing of the Courts and Legal Services Act 1990 and the Access to Justice Act 1999, it seems true to say that the work of solicitors and barristers has changed so much that it is no longer necessary for there to be two separate professions.

The first of these two Acts allowed solicitors for the first time to have higher-court rights of audience by qualifying as solicitor-advocates. The more recent Access to Justice Act 1999 strengthened this process, and solicitors now increasingly advocate in the higher courts such as the High Court and appeal courts. Solicitors are now also qualified to become High Court judges and even QCs.

When the two branches of the legal profession were formed in the nineteenth century, they had very different functions — a barrister represented clients in court whereas the solicitor was 'office-based', and if the client's case needed to be litigated in court it was then handed over to a barrister. Now this 'handing over' is no longer necessary, although it remains true that for most court cases, especially in the Crown and High Courts, it will be barristers who actually represent the client in court.

Thus, it can be argued that there are few differences between the work of the two professions, except that the Bar remains a referral profession. This means that members of the public cannot go to a barrister directly but must first consult a solicitor. Solicitors can perform more types of legal work than barristers, and so it seems clear that we no longer require two separate legal professions.

In comparing this answer to the A-grade response, you can see how much weaker it is. First, the changes to each profession are only mentioned briefly. Although both relevant statutes are referred to, the conclusions are oversimplified, especially the assertion that 'solicitors now increasingly advocate in the higher courts'. There is no evidence to support this claim — rather the reverse, because few of the 2,000 solicitor-advocates regularly represent clients in higher courts.

The historical reference is of limited value, and this answer illustrates a common weakness — the failure to understand the specialised work involved in bringing a case to court, where the work of the barrister and the work of the solicitor are interdependent. The solicitor does not simply 'hand over' the case to a barrister. This answer would just qualify as a grade C (8 marks). The absence of statutory references would bring it down to a grade D.

Question 7

Judges

(a) Explain the process of judicial selection and appointment. (10 marks)

(b) Briefly explain the functions of judges in our legal system. (10 marks)

■ ■ ■

A-grade answer

(a) The criteria for judicial appointment were laid down in the Courts and Legal Services Act 1990, but these were amended by the Tribunals, Courts and Enforcement Act 2007. They are as follows:

- district judge — 5 years' qualification as a solicitor or barrister 'gaining experience by being engaged in law-related activities'
- Recorder — 7 years' qualification as a solicitor or barrister 'gaining experience…'
- circuit judge — 7 years' qualification as a solicitor or a barrister or sitting as a Recorder, or 3 years as a district judge
- High Court judge — 7 years' qualification as a solicitor or a barrister, or 2 years as a circuit judge
- Lord Justice of Appeal — 7 years' qualification as a solicitor or a barrister, but in practice always appointed from High Court judges
- Law Lord — 15 years' qualification as a solicitor or barrister and the holding of high judicial office for at least 2 years

New procedures for judicial appointment were laid down in the Constitutional Reform Act 2005, which established the Judicial Appointments Commission (JAC).

The selection and appointment procedure for district judges, Recorders and circuit judges is broadly the same. Suitably qualified candidates apply to the JAC in response to advertisements. References are checked and shortlisted candidates are interviewed by a panel selected from the JAC. The JAC then recommends suitable candidates to the Lord Chancellor for appointment. The Lord Chancellor may appoint these candidates or refer back to the JAC. The Lord Chancellor may not appoint as a judge anyone not recommended by the JAC.

To become a High Court judge, candidates again must apply to the JAC — references are checked and shortlisted candidates and some of their referees are interviewed by a panel of members of the JAC. Again, successful candidates are recommended to the Lord Chancellor for appointment.

Lord Justices of Appeal are always appointed from the ranks of High Court judges and again the procedure involves application to the JAC. Applicants are interviewed by a panel comprising the Lord Chief Justice and a Head of Division, and the chairperson of the JAC plus a lay member.

Law Lords are drawn mainly from Lord Justices but, since the House of Lords is the supreme UK Court of Appeal, senior Scottish and Northern Irish judges are also appointed. The Lord Chancellor provides one name to the prime minister for recommendation to the queen. This nomination may not be rejected by the prime minister.

> *This is a detailed answer that fully recognises the changes made to judicial selection following the creation of the JAC, and would obtain the full 10 marks.*

(b) The functions performed by judges depend on the court in which they sit. In civil cases, they preside over the trial, hear all the evidence led by both sides and then make a decision, which has to be presented to the parties in detail. If the judge holds the defendant liable, damages will then be determined. In addition, the High Court has the jurisdiction of conducting judicial reviews, which have grown in number considerably in recent years. This requires judges to assess the legality or reasonableness of decisions or actions of public bodies, especially those of cabinet ministers.

In a criminal trial in the Crown Court, the judge has to keep order, decide legal questions such as the admissibility of evidence, direct the jury on the law and sum up the evidence impartially. If the jury finds the defendant guilty, it is then the judge's duty to pronounce sentence.

In both the Court of Appeal and the House of Lords, judges have an important law-making role, through both the doctrine of judicial precedent and statutory interpretation. Cases such as *Attorney General of Jersey* v *Holley*, which changed the law of provocation, or *Hedley Byrne* v *Heller* on recovery of pure economic loss, are good examples of law changes. Such senior judges are also often asked by the government to hold judicial inquiries following a disaster such as the *Herald of Free Enterprise* sinking or the *Piper Alpha* explosion.

> *This answer is succinct and well structured, with a clear sequence in terms of 'ascending hierarchy' of the judiciary. It would be awarded 10 marks.*

Question 8

Alternatives to courts

Briefly explain the alternatives to the courts in the resolution of civil disputes. (10 marks)

■ ■ ■

A-grade answer

At present, there are many options available in dispute resolution: these include administrative tribunals, arbitration, mediation and conciliation. Considerable impetus has been given to arbitration and mediation under the Civil Procedure Rules (CPR), which gave effect to Lord Woolf's civil justice reforms. Courts are now required to ask parties to litigation to consider the possibility of alternative dispute resolution (ADR). If one party unreasonably declines to consider ADR, the court may refuse to award costs if that party succeeds in the action (*Dunnett* v *Railtrack*).

Tribunals have been established over the last 50 years in particular to deal with many different types of problems — employment, social welfare benefits, immigration, fair rent etc. They have a limited jurisdiction, unlike courts, and are presided over by a panel comprising a legally qualified chairperson and two assessors, who, although not legally qualified, are experienced in the area of the dispute. These tribunals now play the largest part in civil dispute resolution as, between them, they hear over 1 million cases a year.

Arbitration has been described as 'privatised litigation' and is the process whereby both parties agree to the appointment of an arbitrator to settle their dispute. This procedure is governed by the Arbitration Act 1996. In many commercial contracts, there is a *Scott* v *Avery* clause, which effectively compels the parties to resolve any contractual dispute through arbitration. There are three different forms of arbitration: small claims with a limit of £5,000 in the County Court; consumer arbitration, using schemes approved by the Office of Fair Trading, involving various trade associations (such as ABTA); and commercial arbitration.

Mediation has become more popular in recent years, having proved its value in the USA. This process involves a neutral mediator working with both parties to assist the parties themselves to reach an agreed solution. No decision is imposed and the parties retain the right to litigate if mediation fails. It is said that while court-based litigation, and to a certain extent arbitration too, is 'rights-based', mediation allows the parties' individual interests to be better represented.

Conciliation can be described as a kind of 'halfway house' between mediation and arbitration. Here, the conciliator, a neutral third party, after discussing the problem between the parties, offers a non-binding opinion to try to resolve the dispute.

section

📝 This is a strong answer. It has an effective introduction, followed by a full and accurate description of each type of dispute resolution with good illustrative examples and clear legal references. This essay would receive the full 10 marks.

■ ■ ■

C-grade answer

There are various ways of resolving a dispute other than through the civil courts:

- Negotiation — this is where the parties discuss the issues of the dispute with each other, either verbally or in writing, in an attempt to resolve their dispute. Usually, the lawyers for both sides carry out this negotiation.
- Mediation — this is where the parties are joined by a mediator, who is an unbiased and neutral third party. He or she listens to both sides and guides them towards an agreed settlement.
- Arbitration — this is where the two parties allow a neutral person to decide the outcome. The arbitrator, who is qualified to resolve the dispute, is appointed by the parties themselves. The parties agree to be bound by the arbitrator's decision. Many consumer problems are resolved using this procedure in the small claims court or through trade bodies.

📝 The contrast with the A-grade answer is stark — this answer is weaker in every sense. There is no statutory authority and the explanations are limited. The failure to refer to tribunals is common and inevitably results in loss of marks. In terms of style, too, the answer is poor — this bullet-point answer style should be avoided unless there is a severe time problem, or a justifiable reason for using a listing technique. This technique almost always results in an unconvincing answer, unless there is additional factual explanation. This answer would receive 5 or 6 marks.